P.E.R.S.U.A.D.E.

P.E.R.S.U.A.D.E.

Communication Strategies That Move People to Action

Marlene Caroselli, Ed.D.

SkillPath Publications
Mission, KS

Project Editor: Kelly Scanlon

Copyeditor: Mason S. Cole

Page Layout: Premila Malik Borchardt

Cover Design: Rod Hankins

ISBN: 1-57294-053-0

Library of Congress Catalog Card Number: 96-67386

10 9 8 7 6 5 4 3 2   00

Printed in the United States of America

Contents

Introduction

The theme of this book is best captured in the words of management guru Ken Blanchard: "The key to successful leadership today is influence, not authority." If successful leadership is indeed dependent on persuasive communications, then today's leaders must continuously improve their influence. The corollary to this authority-reduced role of the leader is the fact that anyone, at any level, can demonstrate leadership, which for the purpose of this book is considered as "the ability to effect positive organizational change."

More than ever, today's leaders, especially those with the word "manager" on their business cards, are experiencing an organizational oxymoron. They have less clout than before, less control over functions because of downsizing, empowerment, self-directed work teams, or outsourcing. And yet, their responsibilities have grown rather than decreased. To succeed, they must develop strong motivational skills. And such skills, of course, are directly related to the ability to persuade others.

While *P.E.R.S.U.A.D.E.* is designed with the business person in mind, the tips and techniques presented will serve you whenever and wherever you find yourself negotiating for win/win outcomes. Whether in a business meeting or bazaar, negotiating a pay raise or a new car, motivating co-workers or community teams, you will—if you follow this advice and work on these activities—find yourself better equipped to deal with the forces that oppose your good intentions.

The book is organized in eight chapters. Each focuses on an adjective depicting one characteristic of persuasive communications. The first letters of each chapter spell the word *persuade*. This easy mnemonic will help you remember the tools that will lead you to success as a leader. Within each chapter are numerous recommendations, exercises, and real-world examples—all illustrating the "hows" to inspire, the "whats" to include, the "whos" to reach, and the "whens" and "wheres" most capable of leaving indelible messages in the minds and hearts of your audience. Note that here the word *audience* is used to mean those you are attempting to persuade or influence— either through your spoken or written words or the example you set with your actions.

Positioned. This chapter examines the several definitions of the word "position," considering it from the advertising perspective and examining the values inherent in a proposal or product. The careless communicator speaks or writes without forethought, but the persuasive communicator knows what impression can be created by placing particular information at the beginning, middle, or end of a message. Those who are skilled at influencing others are attuned to the nuances of language and to the power words possess; they agree with the Greek poet Pindar's observation: "Words have a longer life than deeds."

Engage. Milo Frank asserts that presenters have only 30 seconds to engage a reading or listening audience. Given the limited attention span of the average person, you must find ways to attract and keep your audience's attention if you have any hope of persuading them. A number of these methods and techniques are presented in this chapter, along with exercises that will help you improve your skills in this area.

Realistic. Listeners will join your can-do efforts if your calls to action truly are doable. Pie-in-the-sky schemes are a waste of everyone's time. Your language must not only inspire, it must honestly acknowledge any obstacles that may be encountered. This chapter will provide strategies like the 3-C Approach to help you in two ways. First, you'll learn ways to realistically assess the strength of your viewpoint. And second, you'll learn to decide when to come on strong with your message or when to make a gracious retreat.

Simplified. "Men of few words are the best men." So said Shakespeare in the days when sexist language was acceptable. The sentiment, though, is unassailable. In this era when chaos is king, a simple message will stand out from more complicated messages and help you connect with the audience. Several techniques for simplifying your message are presented in this chapter.

Universal. Persuasive elements that transcend time and place and industry are identified here. These are elements that validate your key points and appeal to your listeners and readers. Certain terms hit the right buttons in your audience and help you connect with them.

Anticipated. Effective persuaders borrow a technique from the world of sports: "The best defense is a good offense." In professional communications, this means introducing an anticipated negative and putting a positive spin on it before your audience can oppose it.

Developed. If presented in a haphazard fashion, the most winning argument loses its impact. In this chapter, you will find the ever-popular patterns for developing your oral and written persuasions, such as subordination, the 5-C Technique, and parallelism.

Energizing. The same "call to action" that concludes the book should conclude every persuasive communication as well. The closing needs to be energizing, specific, and action-oriented. After all, the last thing your audience sees and hears is usually the first thing they will remember.

One

Positioned

The term "positioning" comes from the advertising world. It refers to the persuader's successful efforts to position an idea or product in the mind of the audience. Instead of merely pointing out the advantages of a given item, the persuader, using positioning, first tries to understand which factors might influence this particular audience to accept the item's advantages.

Formal, Core, and Augmented Values

From the advertising world, too, come the terms "formal," "core," and "augmented." They refer to the values in the idea you wish to sell, the proposal you want to make. To illustrate, Charles Revson, the cosmetics king, once observed, "In the factory we make cosmetics, and, in the drugstore, we sell hope." The *formal* value is the obvious one, the typical, the predictable. It's what your audience expects. Formal values are clearly denoted. They are embedded in the saying, "What you see [advertised], is what you get."

The *core* value is the connotative one that allows you to leave an indelible message in the mind of your audience. The core message is more implied than articulated. It is often more symbolic than substantial.

The final value is the *augmented*—a value added, so to speak. If you were a salesperson selling a car to a potential buyer, you might point to a low interest rate in the financing plan. It is peripheral to the actual sale of the car, but is also a persuading factor.

We sometimes give words the Herculean task of invading other people's minds and causing a complete turnaround, a shift in thinking they may have clung to for many years. Words—if personified—can be seen with their ears to the ground, their nose to the grindstone, their shoulders to the wheel, and sometimes their back to the wall.

And yet, we know that a single juror can sometimes sway the thinking of the remaining eleven. We know there are salespeople who belong to "million-dollar" clubs. We know of supervisors who manage to extract extraordinary performances from ordinary employees. We know there are presidents capable of inspiring citizens to give up comfortable lives and join a corps that brags of being "the toughest job you'll ever love."

To understand how they do it, try Exercise #1, which tests your ability to position your proposal in the minds of your co-workers.

P.E.R.S.U.A.D.E.

Distinguishing Among Types of Values

Assume you want the entire office to join you in celebrating National Quality Month (in October of each year). What are some of the values associated with such a celebration? (One is supplied in each category just to get you started.)

Formal

1. Being part of a nationwide effort to improve the quality of goods and services

2. _____

3. _____

4. _____

Core

1. Improving interpersonal relationships

2. _____

3. _____

4. _____

Augmented

1. Bringing in customers to see exactly what we do

2. _____

3. _____

4. _____

Answers

Possible positioning factors for each value might be:

Formal: Improved quality of product

Better customer relations

Opportunity to increase receptivity to TQM

Core: Something new, a chance to do something different

Increased pride among employees

Enriching the culture of the organization

Augmented: Media coverage

Recruitment of new employees

Opportunity to benchmark with others celebrating Quality month

Many different responses are possible for Exercise #1, of course. These very differences, though, suggest that thought has gone into the proposal. Poor persuaders are haphazard presenters of ideas. Effective persuaders, by comparison, have polished presentations. And one technique that will lend polish to your efforts is to consider the *formal*, *core*, and *augmented* values associated with the concept or product you want others to accept. By attending to these values you are, in effect, placing yourself in your listeners' minds. In this "position," you are better able to consider what factors might persuade them to follow your lead.

Inductive and Deductive Reasoning

There is another definition of "position" the convincing communicator needs to think about: "position" in terms of strategic placement. For example, if the topic is a controversial one, you may wish to develop your argument before announcing your intention. When you do this, you are actually using an *inductive* approach to reasoning. You are literally leading others *into* the essence of your position.

Assume, for example, that you are facing the difficult job of firing an employee your superiors regard as an excellent technician. You've decided to explain your action with an internal memo. If you begin by stating your intention—"I have decided to fire Bob Smith"—your manager might read no further, becoming so incensed at the prospect of losing an outstanding employee that rationally following the points you listed after that opening sentence would be impossible.

By contrast, the following inductive line of reasoning would probably convince your boss more readily:

- For sixteen of the last thirty-one working days, Bob Smith has come to work late.

- He has been absent eleven days in the last two months.

- He has taken equipment home without authorization.

- He has worked overtime on four occasions without first obtaining approval.

- He has been seen at the race track on "company time."

- He has had four confrontations with other employees in the last six months, and one of those incidents resulted in a physical attack.

- He has refused to join a process improvement team.

- Two EEO complaints have been filed against him so far this year.

- This month alone, we have received four customer complaints about work he has completed.

- Despite numerous (documented) counseling and coaching sessions, I have seen no improvement in either the accuracy of his work or his attitude toward it.

For these reasons, I have decided to terminate him effective November 1.

The opposite of this inductive style of reasoning is the *deductive*. In it, you literally are leading your audience *from* the essence of your message. It's an effective approach when you want your readers or listeners to sit up and take notice. The deductive style usually begins with a bold statement, and is then substantiated by details (unlike the preceding inductive example, which began with details and led to the bold statement).

Assume you wanted to persuade your co-workers to join you in an "Adopt-a-School" effort. You might begin your (spoken or written) presentation to them with a startling statistic and then move on to the ways employees might work to improve future statistics:

> *Of all high school graduates, in any given year, 700,000 cannot read the words on their diplomas. And in New York City alone, the number of students who do not graduate from the city's high schools is 49 percent. In our city, that figure is 34 percent.*

> *There is much we can do to improve the quality of education. One effort that requires little time or money is to "adopt a school."*

> *By adopting a school, we form a special partnership that allows us to interact with the school's administration, staff, students, and parents in various ways. For example, we can visit classrooms and tell students about career opportunities in our company. Another possibility is to serve as tutors.*

> *The program has enjoyed success. In Spencerport, employees of ABC Company are working with parents to establish a list of "Necessary Future Skills" and to discuss ways parents can help strengthen such skills at home.*

Both inductive and deductive techniques are useful, but they should be used with forethought. The essential question again is: Do you want to lead your audience to your strong position by stating details first, or do you want to state that position first and then lead them from it by supplying substantiating details?

Analysis Assignment

In this exercise, you can test your ability to analyze communications and decide which are the most persuasive—looking only at the strategic placement of various points (all of which are accurate but placed differently).

The situation is this: A manager is trying to persuade her boss to let her attend an upcoming commercial training program. Which of these memos do you find most persuasive? Provide your analysis in the space under each example.

Memo "A"   I would like to attend an Effective Decision-Making seminar that will be held the first week in March. The cost is rather high—$1,500—but it should be worth it. I know the first week in March will be hectic because we will have just submitted our budgets and will need to attend to all the work we didn't get done while concentrating on them. However, the workshop is being held only once this year, in March. My secretary can handle most of my work while I am away.

You know that I intend to move up in this organization and will need to sharpen my decision-making skills so I can handle executive situations. This workshop will prepare me for future promotions. So, if you think the class is valuable, I hope you will sign this request.

Your analysis of this memo: _____

_____

_____

_____

_____

_____

_____

In terms of its ability to persuade, what grade would you give it?

_____

Memo "B"   As you know, I have been looking for ways to gain some skill in dealing with the everyday problems that arise in my position. I think I have found a way to give me the decision-making skills that I lack. ABC University is holding a one-week seminar in early March; the focus is improving decision-making skills. The cost is $1,500. I've checked around and learned that P.R. Septill, head of Purchasing, attended a similar seminar last year and found it valuable. I am certain I will find this one equally valuable if you will just grant me your permission to attend. I need the check voucher by the end of the week.

Your analysis of this memo: _____

_____

_____

_____

_____

_____

_____

In terms of its ability to persuade, what grade would you give it?

_____

Memo "C"   When we met recently for my performance review, you advised me that I needed to develop my ability to make decisions quickly and effectively. I assured you then I would take steps to improve my skills in that area. Consequently, I was pleased to learn ABC University will be presenting a workshop on that very topic, to be held the first week in March. This is an ideal time, as our budgets will have been completed by then. The workshop leader is Morton Stampley, whose book on that topic heads the management bestseller list.

Because the workshop will be held nearby, there will be no additional cost for lodging. Of course, I will take care of my own meals and transportation, so the only charge will be for the workshop itself. And—to make the tuition fee of $1,500 cost-effective for the department—I would be happy to share what I learned with others, either in the form of a report or as a brief presentation during a staff meeting. The enrollment is limited, so I would appreciate your signing this request today.

Your analysis of this memo: _____

_____

_____

_____

In terms of its ability to persuade, what grade would you give it?

_____

Now compare your analysis to the following:

Memo "A"; Grade: D

The memo begins well enough—it is straightforward and specific, although it focuses on "I" rather than "you." The first problem, however, is the immediate admission of the high cost. The persuasion is further weakened by the conditional nature of the writer's opinion of the worth of such an investment: "It *should* be worth it."

The next problem is the writer's concession that she will have a great deal of work piled up during that particular period. (It is never wise to point out to a boss that you are unable to handle multiple priorities. The writer, it seems, completed the budget assignment but allowed everything else to fall behind.)

The most egregious error here is the admission that the secretary can handle most of the manager's work. It makes you wonder why the manager is even needed if the secretary can do the work. It might also cause the reader to think of giving the next pay raise to the secretary instead of to the manager.

The tone of the next paragraph is offensive. It almost seems threatening, at the very least arrogant or overly ambitious. The reader of this memo is left thinking the writer will need much more than a class in decision-making in order to handle executive situations. Further problems lie in the yielding of power to the reader: "So, if *you* think the class if valuable …." Continued erosion of the writer's position can be found in the word "hope": "I hope you will sign this request."

P.E.R.S.U.A.D.E.

Memo "B"; Grade: B-

This memo is better, but the first sentence (26 words) doesn't tell the reader very much except that she doesn't seem to have any expertise in dealing with the problems of her position. (Saying that you are "looking for ways to gain some skill" implies you do not yet possess that skill—a damaging admission.) In the next sentence, the writer also admits she lacks decision-making skills. It serves no good purpose to remind a boss of your inadequacies. The writer is less than positive as she begins to push for the seminar: "I *think* I have found a way." Rather than qualify a statement, it's better to assertively state it: "I have found an excellent course in decision making."

It was better to position the cost in the middle of the memo rather than at the very beginning as the first memo did. However, the cost should be broken down to a per capita cost whenever possible. For example, if the writer had said:

> *Upon my return, I would be happy to share what I have learned with the other members of the department.*

she then could have said:

> *In this way, the actual tuition cost is only $150 for each of us.*

The writer is probably politically astute enough to know there is often competition among heads of departments. Her boss—knowing that the head of Purchasing had received decision-making training— might be more inclined to acquire some of the same for her department.

The near-ending here is poor. It is confusing to state "I am certain I will find this one equally valuable if you will just grant me your permission to attend." The sentence implies that the value of the seminar depends on the boss granting permission. Plus, the tone puts the writer in a subservient position, as if she were begging. The actual ending, however, is strong. In no uncertain terms, it tells the reader what the writer needs. Another sentence might more adequately complete the memo, but as written it is assertive and proactive.

Memo "C"; Grade: A

This is a clever letter. Admittedly, it is longer than the other two, but what it lacks in brevity it more than compensates for with its persuasive content. By reminding the boss of her recommendation to develop particular skills, the writer asserts that she is, in a sense, "following orders." The first two sentences do more: they reflect the employee's willingness to improve and also to provide documentation for the *next* performance review.

Note the positive spin this writer puts on the fact that budgets will be completed by the time of the seminar. She also validates the worth of the seminar by citing the credentials of the instructor. By comparing this seminar to others held out of town, the writer is working to offset potential reluctance to the price. Another step is taken to weaken possible resistance: the writer offers to share the knowledge.

The ending urges the boss to act quickly ("because enrollment is limited"). By saying, "I would appreciate your signing this request today," the writer sounds confident the request will be approved. The only remaining question is whether the request can be signed before enrollment closes. Also, the ending is more "finished" than the one in the preceding example.

Just a note about sounding self-confident. Assume you are a teen-ager living in a family of many drivers but with only one car available. If you ask, "Can I have the car tonight?" your parents will respond either "yes" or "no." However, if you are confident that you can have the car, you give your parents a different question to answer: "Should I have the car back at 8:30 tonight or can I keep it until 9:00?"

P.E.R.S.U.A.D.E.

Not only does Memo C show confidence, it also demonstrates attention to the benefits to be derived. If you examine the memo from the formal, core, and augmented perspectives, you find:

Formal: The employee is working toward a need identified by her manager.

Core: The proposal suggests a willingness to improve.

Augmented: There would be an opportunity for others in the department to learn about the topic if the employee shares what she has learned.

Politics

Office politicking exists. Since there is no easy way around it, consider the good side to office politics: they can make you more sensitive and astute, more aware of the best way to get things done. If, as Vance Packard asserts, leadership is "the art of getting others to want to do something that you are convinced should be done," and if that something is indeed ethical and in the best interests of the organization, then you need to find "best ways."

One method is to become aware of what interests your boss. She may be interested in knowing what other department heads are doing, supporting the organizational mission, ISO-9000, chaos theory, or just her own career. Whatever her interests, if she is the one you must persuade, you will do well to reflect her interests in your proposal if you possibly can. She, in turn, knows what interests her boss. If your proposal has captured that interest, you are again furthering your position.

Knowing about these interests could work not only to your advantage, but also to your boss's—especially if you're able to share information regarding those interests. And—again assuming your position is an ethical one—you can contribute to the organizational emphasis by knowing your manager's values. To avoid "playing politics" is to label yourself politically naive. It's possible to play the political game with an ethical goal in mind and toward a win/win outcome.

It's wise, therefore, to know the rules of the political game and their likely results:

- Support and cooperation from others
- Self-growth as a means to increase your contribution to the organization
- A solid network to expedite communications
- Greater facility in getting work done
- Better teamwork
- The ability to move quickly in times of crisis

A long-held humorous view of success in organizations is that knowledge of your job constitutes 90 percent of that success and the other half is politics! Being politically correct means knowing which way the corporate winds are blowing and using those winds in your sails as you direct positive change in your organization. As your career advances, the amount of scrutiny increases. If you're perceived as someone who isn't able to inspire cooperation, someone who's difficult to work with and for, someone who can't be depended on or whom others can't depend on, then your chances for success will be limited. Remember that one hand washes the other in locations other than sinks!

Place

There's much to be said for being first. This position, if you're successful, virtually guarantees you will be remembered. Should you doubt the truth of these words, think about the first woman to fly solo across the Atlantic. Who was she? Amelia Earhart, of course. Who was the second? Did history even record her name?

While the feat was no less remarkable, by virtue of being second, the individual simply isn't remembered. Being the second one to make a proposal is usually an exercise in futility (unless yours offers something the first one didn't). Keep in mind that being first grants you a position of power you can't get elsewhere.

Common Views of "Position"

Finally, the word "position" should be considered in its most familiar forms. Ask yourself these questions before, during, and after your persuasive efforts.

- Who is in the best position (regardless of job title) to assist you with your efforts?

- What is the company's position on this subject? What has its position been in the past?

- If your proposal is being presented orally, when is the best time to give it?

- Where is the best place?

- Who should sit next to whom?

- If the proposal is being circulated, whose name should appear on the routing list first?

- What are the positions or views held by the various members of your audience?

- Considering these positions, whom should you approach first?
- Whose endorsement of your proposal will depend on the positions of others?
- Who is in a position to defeat your proposal? What would win this person over?
- Who has external support that can increase the likelihood of your proposal being accepted?
- What "buzzwords" should be included in your "position paper"?
- How might the political climate in the community, the industry, or the country affect your proposal?
- Which of your former positions or past duties might lend strength to your proposal?
- What position(s) do you now hold might enhance the proposal?
- What well-respected figure holds a position (on the proposal subject) that is similar to your own?
- Who is in the "rising-star" position, and would this person support your proposal?
- How can you position yourself for the next acceptance you will have to achieve?
- How many others have you attempted to sway to your point of view?
- Are you in a position to alter your proposal if need be?
- How solid is the position of your chief opponent?

Summary Exercise

Here are the key points from this chapter about positioning. Without looking back, list what you remember about each of the terms listed:

1. Positioning (as defined in advertising terms)

   _____

   _____

2. Formal value

   _____

   _____

3. Core value

   _____

   _____

4. Augmented value

   _____

   _____

5. Inductive reasoning

   _____

   _____

6. Deductive reasoning

   _____

   _____

7. Strategic placement of information in a memo

_____

_____

_____

_____

_____

_____

8. Politics

_____

_____

_____

_____

9. Place

_____

_____

_____

10. Positions

_____

_____

_____

_____

Two

Engaging

Remember, you generally have only thirty seconds to capture your audience's attention. This chapter explores some methods for engaging your audience—for capturing and keeping its attention.

The Persuasive Look

Even before you speak or before your written words are read, people are making judgments about you—judgments that can work for or against you. Take a moment to think about some factors that may influence others before you have a chance to persuade them with your oral arguments. How about your written arguments? What factors—other than the actual content of the words—might speak to your audience before you can do so yourself? Neatness? Yes. The quality of the paper? Absolutely. The look of the document (e.g., computer-generated versus a typed copy)? Without question.

Presentation Makes the Difference

Certain specific factors constitute the "look" of a document. How many of these factors can you find as you compare Example A to Example B? Both memos contain the same information, but you probably are drawn to one more than the other. Analyze why.

Example "A"

For Term I, which extends from July 6 to August 27, you will find that the best way to reach me is by calling me at 555-6402 on weekdays (Monday through Thursday only) from the hours of 8:30 a.m. to 4 p.m. I, of course, will be taking a vacation this summer and will be gone from August 19 to September 1. You will be able to reach me in the office on Thursday, September 2. Should serious situations arise which cannot await my return, you should call Susan on campus at 555-7128 or Monica Smith at 555-1756. Because of my own vacation schedule, the days for registering students for Term II will be scheduled for a ten-day period prior to my departure: August 3 to 12.

As far as the CWRT program is concerned, the registration period is scheduled for August 11 and 23. There are two possible ways the packets will be received by the students: the packets will either be mailed out to students or distributed to students in classes on July 25 and 26. Please be advised that no new students may register for WWT-334; this class is only to be filled with current students; new students will be turned away. If there are sufficient students registered for WWT-334 and if there are enough of the less experienced students, the instructor has agreed to try to form a second class for the latter group. I will be stationed at CWRT, Building 232, Room 3 for any registration questions that you may have, during the period of August 11-13. Please be advised that there is no phone in my office. Ergo, if you do have questions regarding the registration process, it will be incumbent upon you to contact me at CWRT.

Analysis

What is your reaction to the information presented here?

_____

_____

_____

Example "B"

Office hours: The best way to reach me is by phone, 555-6402, Monday through Thursday, 8:30 a.m.-4:00 p.m.

Vacation: I will be gone from August 19 to September 1, but you can reach me in the office (by phone) on Wednesday, September 2. In case of emergency, call Susan on campus (555-7128) or Monica Smith (555-1756).

Registration: Due to my vacation, I will be registering students early, from August 3-12. Please note:

- Packets that are not mailed in advance to students will be brought to classes on July 25 and 26.

- No new students may register for WWT-334.

- Dr. Hammar says he will try to blend in the less experienced students with the more experienced ones.

- I will be available in CWRT, Building 232, Room 3 for any registration questions on August 11-13, 8:30 a.m.-12:30 p.m. Remember, I have no phone on base.

Analysis

The "obese" paragraphs in the first example *dissuade* the reader from wanting to delve in and find the message. By comparison, the second memo uses typographical and stylistic aids that invite the reader to read further. Can you list at least five of these aids?

1. _____

2. _____

3. _____

4. _____

5. _____

Answers

Here are some of the typographical aids apparent in the second example:

- Use of topic headings on the left
- Use of italics
- Use of white space
- Use of bullets
- Short sentences
- The introductory sentence that separates the topic from the details

The Persuasive Hook

Assuming author Milo Frank is correct about speakers and writers having only a handful of seconds in which to engage the audience, then you must start your message—spoken or written—with a stylistic device that "hooks" your audience so you can "drag them in." In the verbal haystacks piled around us each day, your "needle" should shine so brightly it can't be missed.

Management guru Peter Drucker defines an age-old communication problem: "Throughout the ages, the problem always has been how to get communication out of information." You have the solution to the problem if you are presenting your information in such a way that the audience gets the point immediately. If you present your intentions directly and deliberately, you'll communicate in a way your audience will appreciate. And appreciation is a prelude to persuasion.

Here are some tips for hooking your audience:

- **Start fast.** If you don't have much time, state your purpose in your introductory remarks. Don't bury it in the middle—your audience may not remain with you long enough to reach the middle.

- **Display the "you" attitude.** After you have completed the first draft of your remarks, scan it quickly and count: How many times does the word "I" appear? How about "you"? In persuasive communications, remember that the focus is on the audience, not on the persuader.

- **Determine the psychological attraction.** Remember Charles Revson separating the product from the emotion (hope, in his case)? Consider what emotion is needed in your particular message. Does your audience need reassurance? Will an appeal to pride be most appropriate? When F. Scott Fitzgerald observed, "You can stroke people with words," he showed an understanding of the psychological underpinnings of persuasion.

- **Open with a bang, not a whimper.** The "bang" could be a question or a quotation or a startling statistic. It could be an anecdote or a twist on the familiar. (Columnist William Safire, for example, once commented, "I have a lot of ironies in the fire.")

- **Make the sound bite the audience.** Sound bites are memorable messages. We find them in courtrooms, in boardrooms, in classrooms, and in the halls of government. Long after the excess verbiage has been forgotten, the sound bite core remains. What does your message sound like? Is it sharp enough to "bite" the reader or listener, to penetrate the many layers of drivel to which he or she is exposed each day?

You may not be able to think of a bit of feisty verbal elegance for every persuasive message, nor would you want to. But there will be times—especially when your persuasive message is an inspirational one—when you want your words remembered. Here's an example: a division of the New Jersey National Guard, responsible for supplying equipment needed by the Army officers and troops, has created this motivational phrase: "We never let our Guard down." Appropriate for both its single and its double *entendre*, the phrase symbolizes the pride the Guard takes in its missions—whether during a foreign crisis or a domestic disaster.

The sound bite can rhyme. It can be alliterative. (If "rock 'n' roll" were "rock 'n' jump," would it have the same appeal? Probably not.) It even can be feisty or funny, manicured or mischievous. Above all else, the sound bite is memorable.

Writing Persuasive Openings

Assume that your boss has asked all employees to put in writing any request for a raise. Write the opening of your persuasive memo here, making sure to include at least one "hook" technique.

Use any one of the "hook" devices presented so far:

- A fast start
- The "you" attitude
- Psychological appeal
- Starting with a bang
- A sound bite

Or use any combination of these to create a "hook" for a persuasive communication.

_____

_____

_____

_____

_____

_____

_____

_____

_____

The Persuasive Line

Now that you have the attention of your audience, you have to keep it. Keeping it means providing arguments that will sway your audience to your line of thinking. Your "engagement" must continue until the end of your communication and beyond, keeping up with *their* concerns. One vital factor you must consider is the WIFM question—one that listeners invariably ask *themselves* (if they don't ask *you*): "**W**hat's **I**n it **F**or **M**e?"

Now's the time for the force of logic. A well-structured argument will answer the question by allowing your cogent points to speak for themselves. Before working on the organizational strategies that follow, develop your "line." Make notes on these tips, and then work them into the organizational strategy of your message.

Here are some tips for lining up your persuasion "ducks":

- ***Answer the WIFM question.*** You should be able to offer clearly specified, sound reasons why your audience should be persuaded.

- ***List big-picture benefits.*** Beyond the WIFM answers individual audience members will be seeking, detail the benefits that will accrue to the larger organization. Big-picture thinking will help your audience members understand urgencies and will enable them to look beyond the here and now.

- ***Be sensitive to turn-offs as well as turn-ons.*** You can immediately tarnish a perfectly good persuasion by making an insulting allusion (intentional or not). There is no defense against offensive remarks.

- **Offer a guarantee.** First, specify (on your planning paper) any fears your audience might have. Then systematically lay out the steps by which you can eliminate those fears. Giving people a way to back out assures them when they worry about the investment (of time, money, energy) you ask them to make. When they know they have little or nothing to lose, they are more likely to commit.

In the business world, a trial period or pilot project often paves the way for full-scale implementation of a plan. The following sample suggestion would be difficult for management to reject:

"Just let me try it for a week. Then, if we find that the number of errors is not decreasing, I'll give it up and try something new."

- **Cite precedents.** Audiences are easier to convince if they know the plan you are proposing has been tried somewhere else and worked. Just as attorneys cite precedents to validate the worth of their arguments, effective persuaders lessen the sense of risk by pointing to the proven merits of a given proposal.

- **Bring in the big guns.** If it's true that a well-known, well-respected, or popular person supports your position, you'll have an easier time convincing your audience. It's not simply your opinion that the proposal is a good one. Instead, you have the direct or indirect validation of someone (or some organization) who is well-respected and admired for various successes.

Organizational Strategies

As you are presenting your persuasive lines, keep in mind that the order in which you present them can mean the difference between swaying your audience and leaving them snoozing.

- ***Topical pattern of organization.*** This technique probably is the easiest of all. It merely asks you to address each of the elements that constitute the body of a topic. For example, if your presentation on management problems were organized in a topical fashion, you would move from one subtopic to another— in no particular order. You might speak of communication problems, quality problems, hiring problems, and so on.

- ***Sequential pattern of organization.*** This method presents steps in a process. They flow logically, explaining how something is done. If you employ this technique, be sure to give it careful thought so your audience won't be confused by a careless omission or an unnecessary inclusion.

- ***Problem-solution pattern of organization.*** This pattern probably is the most popular among business writers and speakers. Quite simply, it states the problem and then offers several possible solutions to it.

- ***Rational pattern of organization.*** Especially useful when you are making a proposal, with this technique you state your position and then give reasons supporting it.

Exercise #5:

Using the Persuasive Line

A. Assume that your boss has asked all employees to write a memo stating why they feel they deserve a raise.

To begin this persuasive communication, use any one—or combination—of the "lining up" devices presented so far:

- The WIFM factor
- Citing the big-picture benefits
- Being aware of "turn-offs" and "turn-ons"
- Offering a guarantee
- Listing precedents
- Bringing in the big guns

_____

_____

_____

_____

_____

_____

_____

_____

_____

_____

B. Look over the notes you've made about the lining-up techniques you chose, and then organize your memo in support of a raise using one of the organizational strategies mentioned earlier:

- Topic
- Sequential
- Problem-solution
- Rational

_____

_____

_____

_____

_____

_____

_____

_____

_____

_____

_____

_____

_____

The Persuasive Sinker

The final requirement of an engaging communication can best be explained using a fishing metaphor. You must give your message the chance to truly "sink in" to the audience's consciousness.

The following five tips will help you take advantage of your final opportunity to reinforce your points. Remember, the last thing you say is typically the first thing your audience remembers.

- *Cite ease of implementation.* Do you know anyone who isn't overworked? Survey after survey reveals the growing anxiety employees feel about the limited amount of time they have to accomplish ever-growing responsibilities. For this reason, you will have to emphasize the ease of implementation if you want your listeners to seriously evaluate your proposal.

- *If they decide too much will be expected of them, they might tune out.* To offset this possibility, stress the simplicity of operation or the minimal commitment of time or money required. Don't sugar-coat, but do ensure that the advantages outweigh the disadvantages.

- *Restate the benefits.* The last part of an engaging message offers a quick restatement of the benefits you outlined in the body of the communication.

- *Make an appeal to the emotions.* The persuasive communicator is aware of psychological motivation and uses it to his or her advantage. Operating on the belief that your persuasive endeavors are geared toward an ethical outcome from which both parties profit, appeal to your audience's emotions.

- ***Call them to action.*** Never leave listeners uncertain about what is expected of them. Use the conclusion of your persuasive message as a call to action. Specify what you want them to do.

- ***End with a bang not a whimper.*** When possible, use a fact, a quotation, a question, or even a visual gimmick to conclude your communication.

Exercise # 6:

Writing Persuasive Conclusions

Assume once again you are preparing a written communication in which you are attempting to persuade your boss that you deserve a substantial pay raise. Use any one of the "sinker" devices presented so far or any combination to create the "sinker" for your persuasive communication:

- Ease of implementation

- Restatement of benefits

- An appeal to the emotions

- A call to action

- Ending with a bang

Use the following space to conclude your memo, doing all you can to ensure your message really sinks in.

_____

_____

_____

_____

_____

_____

_____

_____

Exercise #7:

Do Your Communications Engage Your Audience?

"Persuade" has been defined as the ability to get others to do something, especially by reasoning, urging, or inducement. But if your audience isn't listening to you and you haven't captured its attention, you won't be able to reason, urge, or induce. To see how well you do at getting and holding your listeners' attention, answer the follow questions:

1. I prefer a spontaneous, off-the-cuff style in my persuasive efforts.

   A. As often as possible

   B. Sometimes

   C. I've never really analyzed it.

   D. Rarely

2. I use visual or verbal attention-getters.

   A. Whenever possible

   B. Seldom

   C. Don't really know

   D. Never

3. I like to use a "build up" before launching into my convincing argument.

   A. If appropriate

   B. Seldom

   C. Don't really know

   D. Always

4. I am sensitive to terms that "turn people off."

   A. Being politically correct is a huge hassle.

   B. I'm not always conscious of these terms.

   C. My message is more important than massaging my listeners' egos.

   D. Always

5. I am verbally playful and like to create memorable phrases.

   A. Not my style

   B. Occasionally

   C. Don't really know

   D. Frequently

6. I feel it is manipulative to appeal to the emotions of my audience.

   A. I would never make such an appeal.

   B. It seems manipulative, but I do it anyway.

   C. I've never really thought about it.

   D. If the message is ethical, so are the means.

7. I concentrate only on pointing out the benefits to the individual.

   A. Always

   B. When I think about it

   C. Seldom

   D. Never

8. I stick to the present when trying to persuade and forget about the past.

   A. Whenever I can

   B. Occasionally

   C. Always

   D. Never

9. I try to personalize my message by sharing a personal experience.

   A. Almost always

   B. On occasion

   C. Rarely—it would bore my audience

   D. Never

10. I point out how easy it would be for my audience to adopt the idea I am proposing.

    A. Never

    B. Sometimes

    C. I think they will realize it if they have been attending to my message.

    D. Always

How to calculate and interpret your score

For questions 1, 4, 5, 6, 7, 8, and 10, give yourself four points for D, three points for C, two points for B, and one point for A. For questions 2, 3, and 9, give yourself four points for A, three for B, two for C, and one for D.

- **34 or higher.** If persuasion were an Olympic event, you'd win the gold medal. You're cognizant of what persuasive elements are and consciously employ them in your communications.

- **33 to 28.** For you, the silver medal. You've apparently incorporated a number of successful strategies into your style but need to refine the old and add some new ones to your persuasion repertoire.

- **27 to 22.** A bronze medal for you, indicating you're better than the average persuader but not among the upper echelon of competitors. More practice is needed.

- **Below 22.** Practice all the tips in this chapter and in others. Then periodically ask friends or colleagues for an evaluation to see whether they've noticed any improvement in your style.

Golden responses:

1. D   Rare is the individual who can marshal his or her thoughts with no advance preparation. While spontaneous persuasion carries the sincerity of heartfelt conviction, it usually leaves the persuader thinking afterwards, "Why didn't I think of saying this or that?"

2. A   Whenever possible, use a visual or verbal attention-getter. There are so many stimuli competing for the audience's attention that you must stand out in order to break through the "tune-out" walls people build to survive.

3. A   If appropriate, use an inductive approach to build up your reader's interest, but only if *appropriate*. If your build up isn't arresting, you could lose your listener.

4. D   Always make your language reflect the respect you have for others.

5. D   As frequently as possible, devise a memorable phrase. Your audience can't possibly remember everything you have to say. So take the nuggets of information and fashion them into a rare piece instead.

6. D   Use all appropriate appeals, ensuring your message is ethical and beneficial to all concerned.

7. D   Never concentrate solely on the benefits to the individual. Go beyond to include group considerations.

8. D   Never explore only the present. Use history, other successful examples, and even predictions to round out your presentation.

9. A   Personal experiences are almost always convincing. A caveat, though: Don't overdo it. Some persuaders get carried away and don't realize the eyes of their listeners or readers are becoming glazed.

10. D   Always make it easier for your audience to be persuaded. Living in an overstressed society as we do, you will have to point out how relatively easy it will be for your audience to accept your plan—unless of course you're touting the very difficulty as a selling point. Ads like those for the Peace Corps ("the toughest job you'll ever love") are undoubtedly successful, but in limited circumstances only.

Summary Exercise

Here are the key points from this chapter about engaging your audience. What do you remember (try not to look back) about each of the terms listed?

1. **"The persuasive look."** Instead of a rambling paragraph, use these typographical aids:

   _____

   _____

   _____

   _____

2. **"The persuasive hook."** What do you remember about these tips?

   How to start

   _____

   _____

   The "you" attitude

   _____

   _____

   Psychological appeals

   _____

   _____

"Bangs" and not "whimpers"

_____

_____

Sounds that bite

_____

_____

3. "The persuasive line." What do you remember about these tips?
WIFM

_____

_____

Big picture

_____

_____

Turn-offs

_____

_____

Guarantees

_____

_____

Precedents

_____

_____

P.E.R.S.U.A.D.E.

Big guns

_____

_____

Personal story

_____

_____

4. "Organizational strategies." What do you remember about
these patterns?

Topical

_____

_____

Sequential

_____

_____

Problem-solution

_____

_____

Rational

_____

_____

5. "The persuasive sinker." What do you remember about these tips?

Cite ease of implementation

_____

_____

Restate the benefits

_____

_____

Appeal to your audience's emotions

_____

_____

Call your audience to action

_____

_____

End with a bang

_____

_____

Three

Realistic

You're likely to be more successful at getting your listeners to jump on your bandwagon if you're honest with them about how "doable" or realistic your idea is. This chapter presents strategies designed to help you realistically assess the strengths of your idea and convey them to your listeners or readers.

Atom-Bomb Words

Pearl Strachan cautions: "Handle words carefully, for words have more power than atom bombs."

Words do have power—the power to wound, enlighten, humor, or inspire. Knowing the potential power you have whenever you put words before your audience, it is vitally important to influence by using the most accurate, most commanding, most realistic information possible. Complete Exercise 8 to get an idea of just how powerful your words can be.

Identifying "Atom-Bomb" Words

A. Recognizing Persuasive Words

1. In your experience, what words—used in your organization, community, or culture—constitute "atom-bomb" words? Record a few here.

   _____   _____   _____

   _____   _____   _____

2. What words constitute "buzzwords" to which your management seems committed?

   _____   _____   _____

   _____   _____   _____

3. What words constitute "stroking"—appropriate for smoothing ruffled feathers?

   _____   _____   _____

   _____   _____   _____

4. What words convey concern for the customer's satisfaction?

   _____   _____   _____

   _____   _____   _____

5. What other category do you think is important?

_____

What are some words strongly identified with this category?

_____   _____   _____

_____   _____   _____

B. Realistic Assessments

Making the difficult decisions about which words to use and which facts to present begins with a realistic appraisal of the situation. Think of a situation from your professional life that calls for persuasion on your part. Outline it here.

_____

_____

_____

_____

_____

_____

C. Evaluating Your Proposal

Now answer these questions concerning the situation you have described:

1. What is the likelihood the other person will agree to do what you wish?

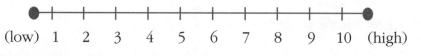

(low) 1   2   3   4   5   6   7   8   9   10   (high)

2. What is the likelihood the other person will have to invest only a minimal amount of resources in order to do what you wish?

(low) 1   2   3   4   5   6   7   8   9   10   (high)

3. What is the likelihood the other person will have to undergo only a minimal amount of change?

(low) 1   2   3   4   5   6   7   8   9   10   (high)

4. How committed are you to the idea or proposal you will present to others?

(low) 1   2   3   4   5   6   7   8   9   10   (high)

5. What degree of correlation is there between your proposal and the firm's mission?

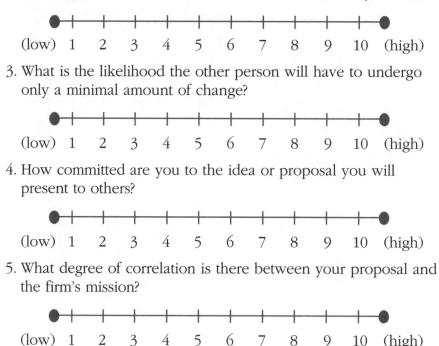

(low) 1   2   3   4   5   6   7   8   9   10   (high)

6. How much experience have you had in the area the proposal focuses on?

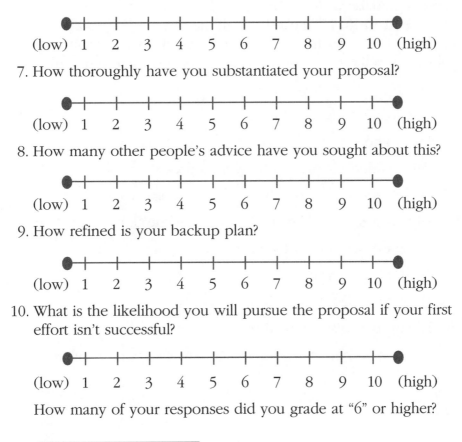

    (low) 1   2   3   4   5   6   7   8   9   10 (high)

7. How thoroughly have you substantiated your proposal?

    (low) 1   2   3   4   5   6   7   8   9   10 (high)

8. How many other people's advice have you sought about this?

    (low) 1   2   3   4   5   6   7   8   9   10 (high)

9. How refined is your backup plan?

    (low) 1   2   3   4   5   6   7   8   9   10 (high)

10. What is the likelihood you will pursue the proposal if your first effort isn't successful?

    (low) 1   2   3   4   5   6   7   8   9   10 (high)

How many of your responses did you grade at "6" or higher?

_____

If you graded more than five responses low, you probably haven't given sufficient thought to the complexity and/or sacrifice your proposal will entail. Before you proceed, analyze it further, perhaps even soliciting the input of those you know to be talented persuaders, or people who've had extensive experience influencing others toward positive ends.

Eleven Reasons a Proposal Can Fail

If you're familiar with the David Letterman show, you have no doubt seen the "Top 10" list. Read through the following "Top Eleven" list of some of the reasons persuasive efforts fail. As you review them, consider whether they could affect any of your own proposals.

1. The goal isn't clearly established.

2. The goal is overly ambitious.

3. There's no realistic consideration of obstacles.

4. Benefits don't outweigh the work involved.

5. There's no analysis of why similar proposals failed.

6. The proposer isn't prepared to address questions that will arise.

7. The proposer doesn't take psychology/politics into account.

8. The timing is wrong.

9. The wrong people are involved.

10. The proposer isn't trusted or liked.

11. The proposer hasn't done enough advance work to sell the idea.

P.E.R.S.U.A.D.E.

Pinpointing Potential Areas for Failure

Consider now an idea or initiative you would like to propose to others (select one different from the one you gave on page 53). The idea, of course, doesn't exist in isolation—it exists within the context of several conditions that surround the idea.

Answer the following questions (and possibly others) that co-exist with the elements of the idea itself. Then lay out your description of the idea. Once you have the description, juxtapose the eleven reasons why a proposal can fail with your proposal description.

A. I would like to persuade:
- ☐ a family member.
- ☐ a co-worker.
- ☐ my boss.
- ☐ a neighbor.
- ☐ other.

B. This is my idea: _____

_____

_____

_____

_____

_____

_____

C. Now answer "True of my plan" or "Not true of my plan" to see if the following negatives might apply to your idea.

	True of my plan	Not true of my plan
1. The goal isn't clearly established.	_____	_____
2. The goal is overly ambitious.	_____	_____
3. There's no realistic consideration of obstacles.	_____	_____
4. Benefits don't outweigh the work involved.	_____	_____
5. There's no analysis of why similar proposals failed.	_____	_____
6. The proposer isn't prepared to address questions that will arise.	_____	_____
7. The proposer doesn't take psychology/politics into account.	_____	_____
8. The timing is wrong.	_____	_____
9. The wrong people are involved.	_____	_____
10. The proposer isn't trusted or liked.	_____	_____
11. The proposer hasn't done enough advance work to sell the idea.	_____	_____

The 3-C Approach

Compel

Different situations call for different persuasion tactics. If you think about it in realistic terms, you'll probably agree that there are times when you're completely in the right. In such situations, you have the upper hand, so to speak, and can afford to use a *compel* strategy, the first of the three "C" strategies.

When you use the *compel* strategy, you can use words that are a little stronger, a little more assertive than usual. You can afford to be a little less apologetic or explanatory. A compelling stance does not mean you should coerce or force others to your viewpoint. Rather, you can expedite the persuasion process because you have the advantage. Persuasive efforts that are compelling can address the point more readily because less "build-up" time is required to develop a persuasive argument.

Concede

Influencers who don't have the upper hand must tread a little more softly. The *concede* strategy might include flattery or praise or humility, depending upon the psychological needs of the individual you wish to persuade. The *concede* strategy works when you're not at an advantage and therefore expect to have to work harder to overcome resistance.

This strategy includes careful development of your position, an anticipation and delicate rebuttal of the target's likely opposition, and a convincing presentation of the benefits to your targeted audience.

When you concede, you may have to admit a negative about yourself or your plan in order to ultimately obtain a positive response. This stance *might* also include admission of past wrong judgments or concessions about the riskiness of your proposal.

Compromise

The most successful persuasions aren't conducted in an us-versus-them atmosphere. When you're willing to make trade-offs (as opposed to being adversarial), the *compromise* approach works best. Using logic and well-substantiated reasons puts you in a better bargaining position. Compromise when neither you nor the other party has the clear advantage, when neither you nor the other party stands to win or to lose a great deal. Use compromise when you need to discuss, not when you need to deal.

P.E.R.S.U.A.D.E.

Can You Identify the Cs in the 3-C Approach?

Three persuasive communications follow, each of which reflects a different persuasive strategy. As you read, fill in the word *compel*, *concede*, or *compromise* to describe the method employed. The situation is this: The speaker wants to take his vacation during the first week in July, when his wife will also have her vacation.

Presentation #1: As you know, Mr. Forrest, I have not taken my scheduled vacations for the past three years. You'll remember that we always seemed to have a crisis arise whenever it was time for me to take off. I willingly put the company's priorities above my own, especially because I had no particular plans to go anywhere. I was happy to take an occasional day off here and there to make up that vacation time.

This year, however, I *have* made plans. My wife will be taking the same two weeks off and we plan to go to Hawaii to celebrate our tenth wedding anniversary. I'm advising you of my plans well in advance so that—should another crisis arise—you can make plans to have someone else cover the situation.

Which "C" strategy was used?

_____

Presentation #2: I have been thinking about the vacation scheduling, Mr. Forrest, and I think I have found a way to make it equitable for everyone. If you have twenty minutes to spare, I'd like to go over my plan with you. It will ensure that we're all—including you and me—able to take the days we're scheduled to take. If we can just have a reserve column of employees to cover for emergencies, then I think we can virtually guarantee equity in the vacation schedule. Let me know your reaction to what I've worked out.

Which "C" strategy was used?

_____

Presentation #3: Jon, remember when you were going through that burn-out period, when you had been working too hard and the stress was really getting to you? Then you went away for two weeks and somehow you found the key for coping with all those production problems? Remember? And when you came back, you looked and acted like a different man. It was as if twenty years had slipped away and you had a new, invigorated response to everything.

Well, I think I'm going through the same kind of stress-induced burnout right now. I need a vacation, Jon. I need to find what you found.

Which "C" strategy was used?

_____

Analysis

The first presentation uses a *compel* style, appropriate because the persuader has the advantage. Knowing that he might encounter resistance from his boss, the speaker suggests that the boss might be violating certain organizational norms by calling upon the speaker to deal with crises even though he's supposed to be on vacation. He's also firmly stating that he's determined to leave as scheduled this year, and that the boss should plan on having other employees deal with the fires that will probably need to be put out.

The *compromise* strategy is evident in the second example. We find the writer is using a professional, mature tone. He isn't demanding. (Notice the use of the word "if." It implies a conditional rather than a commanding style.) The speaker appears to be more concerned with organizational goals than personal benefit—the situation in which compromise works best.

The final situation clearly employs an emotional appeal in its *concede* strategy. The speaker is using flattery as well as a ploy for sympathy as he attempts to persuade the boss of the importance of a vacation. By reminding the boss of how the vacation revived the boss's flagging spirits, the writer is in essence implying that he deserves as much spirit-renewal as the boss.

Real-World Example of a Persuasive Communication

The realistic nature of persuasive communications is captured in a real-world example from the Naval Surface Warfare Center, Port Hueneme Division at Dam Neck, Virginia. In their proposed plan to senior management, the "Visionary Group" realistically addresses the objections it is likely to encounter. The "Visionary Group" consists of Sonnie Blaize, James Brown, Raquel Jackson, Cdr. Marcia Perry, Sylvia Primm, Maria Ruckman, and Calvin Thomas.

Section III

It is said that when the rate of change outside the organization is greater than the rate of change within, then we are observing the beginning of the end of that organization. Therefore, a "take charge" philosophy must be the inspiration for reorganizing NSWC PHD ECO.

A series of actions was undertaken to achieve our objective. Regarding anticipated objections, the following questions were addressed.

1. What objections can be anticipated?
2. What reasons can we expect to hear concerning why reorganization will not work?

Anticipated Roadblocks

1. Authority will be reduced and/or status lost.
2. It will take too long.
3. What good will it do to reorganize?
4. It will have a negative impact on civilian grade levels.
5. There will be a reduction in force.

How will the Visionary Group counter the above roadblocks?

Countermeasures

1. Reduced authority and/or loss of status may be required for efficiency of the new organization. However, new authorities and status will be gained in the new organization.
2. The plan is to expedite the process of reorganization to conclusion.
3. The question of what good will reorganization do will be addressed as a benefit.

4. The response to the question of negative impact on civilian grade levels is the same as #1.

5. Reduction in force is to be avoided.

Benefits

1. A more streamlined "virtual matrix" organization

2. Greater flexibility in task dissemination

3. More efficient use of resources

4. Improved horizontal and vertical communication

5. Morale boost

6. Excellent training for personnel and prospective project managers

7. Better awareness of customer needs

8. Less trauma for personnel when project terminates

9. Increased job satisfaction

10. Career enhancement

11. Better clarification of project objectives

Classifications that will be affected by the change

1. People: All organizational personnel will be positively affected.

2. Departments affected: Marketing, project management, production, test and engineering, financial management, management information services, command services, and process management.

3. Processes: All existing organizational processes will be affected in a positive way.

4. Equipment: Impact on existing equipment will be apparent.

5. Contractors: Current and future contracts will be evaluated on their ESEI level capabilities.

We have developed a chart depicting the proposed "virtual matrix" organizational structure proposed by the Visionary Group and its plan for implementing the project goal. With management's concurrence, the group will provide assistance to the Demographic Quality Management Board in formulating a preliminary strategy for optimizing the benefits to be realized through reorganization.

Summary Exercise

These are the key points from this chapter about realistic persuasion. What do you remember (try not to look back) about each of the terms listed?

1. Atom-bomb words vs. other types of words _____

   _____

   _____

   _____

2. How many of the ten questions about "realistic assessment" do you recall? _____

   _____

   _____

   _____

   _____

   _____

   _____

   _____

   _____

   _____

   _____

   _____

3. The eleven reasons why a proposal can fail _____

_____

_____

_____

_____

_____

_____

_____

_____

_____

4. "The 3-C Approach" _____

_____

_____

_____

Compel. _____

_____

_____

_____

Compromise. _____

_____

_____

_____

_____

Concede. _____

_____

_____

_____

_____

Simplified

People today are bombarded with information at every turn—from billboards to television to the Internet. Advertisers even rent ad space on the stalls of public restrooms! Because of this information overload, simple messages are often the most persuasive. This chapter presents several techniques that will help you keep your message simple—and make it stand out above all the rest.

Try Exercise #11 on the next page to get a quick idea of how simply you present your messages. The rest of the chapter offers suggestions and techniques for keeping all your communications clear and simple.

Exercise #11:

Do I Speak Simply?

"I want no more than to speak simply, to be granted that grace."
George Seferis has expressed a sentiment many people probably feel.
How simply do you speak (and write)? Here is a "simple" quiz to
help you find the answer.

	yes	no
1. I believe big words are indicative of a person's intelligence.	_____	_____
2. I like to pack as much as I can into each sentence.	_____	_____
3. I like to get right to the point—usually in the first sentence.	_____	_____
4. I like my sentences to all be about the same length.	_____	_____
5. I tend to rely on favorite words that I use repeatedly.	_____	_____
6. I always abide by grammatical rules.	_____	_____
7. I believe sentences that are very short sound childlike, so I avoid them.	_____	_____
8. I like the uniform look of paragraphs that all have about the same number of lines.	_____	_____

9. I believe I should use unfamiliar words to help others learn new words.   _____   _____

10. I typically average one preposition for every five words.   _____   _____

(*Note:* You may have to review some of your own correspondence. Count the total number of words in each of six sentences. Then count how many prepositions are in each sentence. This will give you a ratio. For example, if you have 15 words in the first sentence and three prepositions, your ratio is 3 to 15, or 1 in 5.)

Analysis

If the majority of your responses (six or more) were "no," give yourself a pat on the back. You seem to know the impact simplicity can have on your audience. If you had nine or ten "no" answers, give yourself two pats. You definitely know the importance of Einstein's words: "Make everything you do simple—but not simpler [than it has to be]."

Want a closer look at why "no" was the better response? Read on for the explanation of each item:

1. Big words usually reflect the persuader's desire to impress rather than express. The military insists on uncomplicated messages ("Keep it simple, silly!"—the K.I.S.S. Principle). So should you.

2. The general rule is one point per sentence. Your sentences should average about 15 words.

3. If you need to startle your audience, it's appropriate to make your point in the first sentence. Usually, though, you'll need to transition into the focus, by using a sentence or two to build up the audience's receptivity or to tear down preconceptions.

4. Your sentences should vary in length. This helps to spice up your message.

5. We all have favorite words, but they quickly become tiresome to an audience. Use a thesaurus to avoid the tendency to repeat.

6. On occasion, bend those rules, particularly if you're trying to achieve a conversational tone. In persuasive attempts, it's perfectly acceptable to have some sentences that actually are non-sentences. It may be appropriate to end a sentence with a preposition or to say "who" instead of "whom."

7. Short sentences convey weight. ("Words are like sunbeams," it has been said. "The more condensed they are, the more deeply they burn." Don't bury the critical points of your presentation under the "dead" weight of too many words.)

8. If your paragraphs are all the same length, you'll create a tedium that may turn your audience's attention to more interesting topics. Vary both your sentence length and your paragraph length.

9. Unless you *are* a teacher, your mission on Earth isn't to educate others about the wonder of words. Use familiar words and avoid jargon or technical terms if you truly wish to get your point across.

10. Research shows that the best writers have a ratio of one preposition to every eleven words.

The Rule of 7

Psychologists have long agreed that the number "7" possesses a memorable, if not magical, quality. Think of all the famous associations the number has: dwarves and habits and wonders of the world. Seas and sins and telephone-number digits. There are also these well-known "sevens":

- 7 Apostles of Spain

- 7 Churches of Asia

- 7 Hills of Rome

- 7 Summits (highest mountain peaks)

- 7 Ecumenical Churches

- 7 Days of Creation

- 7 Brides for 7 Brothers

- 7 Deacons ordained by the apostles to administer to the poor

- 7 Gifts given with baptism (wisdom, understanding, counsel, fortitude, knowledge, piety, fear of the Lord)

- 7 Wonders of the Ancient World

People can, it seems, efficiently remember seven separate facts or numbers fairly easily. The recall factor applies as well to persuasive communications. When you try to simplify your influencing efforts try this division:

- **3** points to explain why your proposal is needed

- **4** advantages to your proposal

Graphically, your "Rule of 7" looks like this:

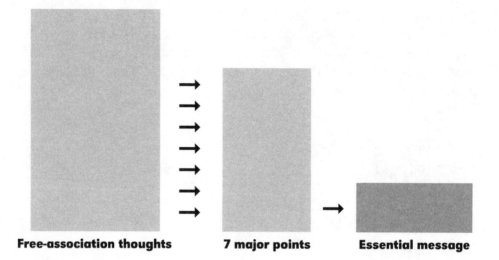

Free-association thoughts   **7 major points**   **Essential message**

The Rule of 7—which takes about 7 minutes to map out—will enhance your persuasive efforts.

Complete Exercise #12 to get a concrete idea of how the Rule of 7 works.

Mapping Out the Rule of 7

Think of an upcoming situation in which you would like to persuade someone to do something. Describe it by completing the blanks in the following sentence.

I would like to persuade _____ to _____

_____

_____

Step 1: Free associate.

Now, in the spaces below, write down your thoughts about the situation you have just depicted. Don't worry at this point about spelling or grammar or logic or being politically correct. Simply let your mind gather its thoughts (some of which may be unrelated) about the person, the prompt, and the circumstances. _____

_____

_____

_____

_____

_____

_____

_____

_____

_____

Step 2: Distill to 7 essential points.

Next, look over what you've written and reduce it to seven major points. List them here.

3 points to explain why your proposal is needed:

_____

_____

_____

4 advantages to your proposal:

_____

_____

_____

_____

Step 3: Distill to your essential message.

The process of refinement continues. As you review your seven essential points, boil them down further into an essential message. Write this new reduced point here: _____

_____

Your distilled message is suitable for both the beginning and the end of your persuasive argument.

Simple Words Are Best

It's difficult to lead others if you can't make them understand where you're going. In the words of James Hayes of the American Management Association, "Leaders who are inarticulate make us all uneasy." Look at this example of a corporate communication and try to determine what it's saying:

> The management of this corporate entity, after due and deliberate contemplation of discrete regrettable practices of which we have recently been made cognizant, is desirous of again directing to your cerebral cognition for consequent consideration the fact—which has, of course, been pointed out on several previous occasions but which, nevertheless, has apparently been overlooked or ignored by an all-too preponderant proportion of our existing employee representation—that all members of this firm should make an earnest, sincere, continuous, and persistent effort to eschew and avoid all excessive lexical expressions, repetitive phraseology, unnecessarily complicated syntax, and lengthy, involved, or obfuscating paragraphs in the process of transmitting internal communication of any nature whatsoever to one or more recipients within the corporate context.

One possible translation would be:

> *"Keep your internal communications simple and easy to read."*

Sometimes persuaders speak and write in a convoluted fashion because they want you to be confused—perhaps because your reaction will be mollified somewhat by a lack of comprehension. Such is the situation in the following statement a manager wrote to an employee:

"Due to inclement climactic conditions in the corporate atmosphere, and in conjunction with the insistence on austerity emanating from the uppermost echelons of our scalar chain, it is incumbent upon me to advise you that—political vagaries and idiosyncratic predilections aside—your solicitation for remuneration that exceeds the annual allotment cannot be granted under the contemporaneous confines that inure to us all."

"I don't get it," replied the confused employee.

"Exactly right," confirmed the manager.

Exercise #13:

Can You Separate the Euphemistic From the Actual?

In the left-hand column, you will find real-world euphemisms that dance around the truth. On the right are the more honest expressions. Can you get a perfect match?

Doublespeak

1. Safety-related occurrence
2. Eliminate redundancies in the human resource area
3. Enhance the efficiency of operations
4. Take appropriate cost-reduction actions
5. Impact attenuation devices
6. Candidate lacks a positive reference input
7. Economically nonaffluent
8. Unlawful or arbitrary deprivation of life
9. Poorly buffered precipitation
10. Terminal living
11. Negative contributions to profits
12. Urban transportation specialist
13. Personal preservation flotation device
14. Ballistically induced aperture in the subcutaneous environment

Translation

A. Bullet hole
B. Cab driver, bus driver
C. Dying
D. Killing
E. Public doesn't like him
F. Fire employees
G. Fire employees
H. Accident
I. Fire employees
J. Life jacket
K. Poor
L. Acid rain
M. Lose money
N. Oil drums placed around highway obstructions

Answers

1. H	6. E	11. M
2. F, G, or I	7. K	12. B
3. F, G, or I	8. D	13. J
4. F, G, or I	9. L	14. A
5. N	10. C	

From "Blah" to "Rah": Use Needed Words Only

The bard probably said it best, "Men of few words are the best men." Don't waste your audience's time with things that don't have to be said. You dilute your message, diminish its force, and distract or pad your primary thought when you add unnecessary words.

To illustrate:

"It is the opinion of this writer that a vote needs to be taken." (14 words)

is simply not as effective as:

"We have to vote." (4 words)

Be on the lookout for padded phrases in your own writing. Strip them, when you find them, down to their bare essentials. Transform bland messages that say, "Blah, blah, blah" into communications your audience will cheer for their clarity. Circling around the point makes the audience impatient. And the more impatient they are, the less receptive they will be to you as messenger.

It's your turn now. Try Exercise #14 to see how well you can spot wordy phrases.

Striking Out Wordiness

Replace the wordy phrases with simplified expressions.

1. Add an additional _____

2. Am acquainted with _____

3. At the present time _____

4. At the time that _____

5. Despite the fact that _____

6. On behalf of _____

7. Important necessities _____

8. In the event that _____

9. In the immediate vicinity of _____

10. In view of the fact that _____

11. Make the acquaintance of _____

12. Pursuant to _____

Tautologies

Tautologies are careless expressions. They contain wasted words. An example is the writer who put out a memo to encourage car-pooling, addressing it to "commuters who drive back and forth to work every day." The fact that they drive "back and forth to work every day" is what *makes* them commuters. The phrase is a tautological expression—it contains self-evident words. It complicates, rather than simplifies, itself.

Keep your eyes and ears open for these expressions, such as "true facts" (if it weren't true, it wouldn't be a fact) or "qualified expert" (a non-qualified person surely can't be an expert). Here are other examples:

- Written correspondence
- Past history
- Waving in the air
- I saw it with my own eyes.
- New innovation
- Real people
- I was thinking in my head.
- Unsold inventory
- Woolly sheep
- Consensus of opinion

The Magic of Metaphors

Used by world figures (Winston Churchill's "Iron Curtain" or Ronald Reagan's "Evil Empire"), the metaphor simplifies a potentially complex and thorny issue by way of a vivid image.

How can you create your own metaphor? How can you weave it into your communications to leave a sharper, more salient image in your audience's mind? Think first of a *thing*—something that grows, a vehicle or animal or game or sport. Something that people eat or do, anything. Next list all the attributes associated with what you have chosen. You will consequently weave those associations into the fabric of your speech.

Jesse Jackson, in his 1984 presidential bid, used the metaphor of the quilt his grandmother made from patches to illustrate the unity that can be achieved by disparate patches sewn together. The comparison was a powerful one.

A technical specialist used the following metaphor to persuade his co-workers to undertake additional training. Its tone is informal, as was the setting. The specialist was trying to influence others he had no real authority over.

> Sometimes when I think about our department, the image of a rowboat comes to mind. The problem with this rowboat is that— even though everyone is rowing very hard, the boat is not moving in the direction it should. The reason is that we're all using different oars, so to speak, and some of us don't even *have* oars.

The only way for us to work more efficiently, I think, is to have training that gives us common standards so we are all using the same method and the most efficient method. It's nobody's fault—we were all hired at different times and as a result, we bring different approaches to the work. I really believe—and I hope you'll agree—that we need uniformity here. Otherwise, we'll never win the race. We might not even make it to shore!

Creating Your Own Metaphor

A. Think of some person or group you would like to influence toward a positive goal. Describe that goal here. What action would you like to see as a result of your persuasion?

_____

_____

_____

B. Now isolate some aspect of the would-be achievement. Choose the goal itself, perhaps, or the struggle to achieve it. Or you might choose you as the influencer or the other person(s) as the influenced. You could even choose the interpersonal dynamics or an intangible such as pride. Write here what aspect you will use for the comparison: _____

_____

C. Next, choose the image that you will tie in to the aspect you chose in B. It can be a plant or animal or mode of transportation—whatever you wish. Write your selection here. It will become the basis for your metaphor. _____

_____

D. Think of what is associated with your selection. For example, if you had chosen the sun as your metaphoric selection, five associations might be:

- The rays of the sun

- The intensity of heat generated by the sun

- Sun spots

- The Earth revolving around the sun

- Eclipses

It's your turn now. Write five (or more) attributes relating to your metaphoric selection.

1. _____

2. _____

3. _____

4. _____

5. _____

E. Your final job is to integrate the metaphorical comparisons into the communication you will use to influence others to a goal you believe is important. Try it here.

_____

_____

_____

_____

_____

If your metaphor is a poignant one, it will remain in your audience's mind long after you deliver your message.

Structuring—From Grab to Tab

In a previous example, the technical specialist began his argument with a metaphor to capture his audience's attention. He focused their thoughts on the picture of a rowboat, causing them to guess about its possible meaning. The metaphor works well, not only in the beginning of a persuasive communication but throughout. Its placement, however, must be deliberate, not offhand. The point? There's an orderly method to presenting every message—whether you're using a metaphor or some other technique.

An easy refrain that will help you structure your persuasions simply but powerfully is this:

- *Grab.* Capture the audience's attention from the "get go."

- *Fab.* Discuss at least one "fabulous" benefit your proposal will lead to.

- *Nab.* Seize upon your audience's natural willingness to make things better rather than worse.

- *Tab.* Tabulate (summarize) the key elements of your proposal.

Structuring Your Communications

1. Let's assume you are a first-level supervisor and you want to persuade your boss to let you attend meetings that typically only midlevel managers attend. What is something you could say that would *grab* her attention? (It could be a quote or a statistic or a question or some work-relevant fact—anything that would pique your boss's interest.)

_____

_____

_____

_____

2. The next step in this simple communication structure is *fab*. What would be one fabulous consequence of the proposal you are making? What is a possible outcome that would please virtually everyone involved?

_____

_____

_____

_____

_____

3. The third element in this "quick-and-clean" strategy is to rope in the listener. Use psychology. Determine which emotional button—if you pushed it—would most likely spur action.

_____

_____

_____

_____

_____

_____

4. Finally, use your concluding remarks to tabulate the pivotal points in your communication.

_____

_____

_____

_____

_____

_____

_____

_____

_____

_____

_____

Summary Exercise

Here are the key points from this chapter about the importance of simplicity in persuasion messages. What do you remember (try not to look back) about each of the terms listed?

1. Do you recall the two categories of "the Rule of 7"? (The first has three items in it and the second has four.)

_____

_____

_____

_____

Step 1: What is the first thing to do as you apply the Rule of 7?

_____

_____

_____

_____

Step 2: What should you do next?

_____

_____

_____

_____

_____

Step 3: What is the final "product" of this three-step process?

_____

_____

_____

_____

If you were to draw the steps of this rule, what would the image be?

2. Separating euphemisms from their real meanings

_____

_____

_____

_____

3. Tautologies

_____

_____

_____

_____

_____

4. Metaphors

_____

_____

_____

_____

5. What are the four stages of going from "grab to tab," and what should you do in each?

_____

_____

_____

_____

_____

_____

_____

_____

_____

_____

Five

Universal

Certain persuasive elements have universal appeal; they transcend time, place, and diverse audiences. This chapter discusses several of those universal "hot buttons" and explains how to use them to connect with your listeners and readers.

Universal Reversal

Certain emotions are experienced universally—love, hate, anger, and joy, among others. No matter who we are, where we live, how old we are, or what we do, we all experience grief at some point, and know what excitement is. The effective persuader understands the importance of these feelings in the influencing process.

The "Universal Reversal" chart on page 97 will help you to deliberately think about what your audience may be feeling and how you can capitalize on or overcome those feelings. If the feelings are negative, you often can reverse them by focusing on other, equally powerful emotions. If the feelings are positive, of course, you can capitalize on them to persuade your audience.

Here's how to use the chart. Start by writing your persuasion objective on the top line. Next, fill in the four columns:

- What are the *main ideas* related to your objective?

- How will your audience react to each?

- What *emotion* will you stress in your response? (Will you have to *R*everse the negative or *U*nite the positives?)

- What degree of *agreement* is likely?

(*Note:* If the likelihood of agreement is less than 50 percent, consider additional emotions that can be stressed. If it is greater than 50 percent, work on polishing the delivery rather than on using an emotional appeal.)

To illustrate, if you are attempting to persuade fellow employees to adopt a "Dress-Down Friday" policy, one of your main points might be "comfort." The reaction, you suspect, might be a feeling of awkwardness, so you would draw an arrow to that word in the second column. At this point, you should take into account a universal emotion that you could use to combat the feeling of awkwardness that others might feel wearing casual clothes to work—even if only once a week.

This might lead you to the word "inclusion" in the next column. If, for example, you cited statistics showing how many corporations now permit employees to work in casual clothes on Fridays, it might help your audience feel it is part of a national movement, that such attire is not unique to their profession but is embraced by many others.

Universal Reversal Chart

Objective: _persuade others to adopt "Dress-Down" Friday_

Main ideas	How will audience react?	What emotion can be stressed?		What degree of agreement is likely for each main idea?
(Draw an arrow from each main idea to at least one emotion your audience will have.)	(Draw an arrow from their emotion to the emotion that you will stress in the next column.)	(For each, determine if you must "reverse" [R] or if you will stress "unity" [U].)		(Express it in terms of a percentage.)
1. _comfort_	fear	fear	R/U	1. ___%
	friendship	friendship	R/U	
	pride	pride	R/U	
	awkwardness	awkwardness	R/U	
	protectiveness	protectiveness	R/U	
	love	love	R/U	
2. _____	hate	hate	R/U	2. ___%
	harmony	harmony	R/U	
	pity	pity	R/U	
	defensiveness	defensiveness	R/U	
	embarrassment	embarrassment	R/U	
	rejection	rejection	R/U	
3. _____	inclusion	inclusion	(R)/U	3. _75_%
	peacefulness	peacefulness	R/U	
	cooperation	cooperation	R/U	
	nervousness	nervousness	R/U	
	surprise	surprise	R/U	
	horror	horror	R/U	

You would, in effect, be "reversing" ("R") a negative feeling into more positive ones by appealing to the universal need to feel part of a larger community. So persuasive is this feeling of being included that you would probably realize more than 50 percent agreement on this point.

"Speech is power," Ralph Waldo Emerson asserted. "Speech is to persuade, to convert, to compel." Attending to the "universal" and "reversal" attributes of your communication will help you to persuade, convert, and compel.

Exercise # 17:

Putting the Universal Reversal Chart to Work

Now that you've had a chance to see how the "Universal Reversal" chart works, you can apply it to any one of the following persuasive situations. Choose the situation that comes closest to a real-life situation of your own and use the complete chart to determine the best way to emphasize the universal prompts to which people respond.

- **Situation A.** You are attempting to persuade a colleague that your way of doing spreadsheets is actually easier and faster than her way.

- **Situation B.** You are trying to persuade your students to spend more time on homework and less time on television.

- **Situation C.** You are trying to persuade a patient to give up smoking.

- **Situation D.** Select a situation of your own.

Universal Reversal Chart

Objective: _____

Main ideas	How will audience react?	What emotion can be stressed?		What degree of agreement is likely for each main idea?
(Draw an arrow from each main idea to at least one emotion your audience will have.)	(Draw an arrow from their emotion to the emotion that you will stress in the next column.)	(For each, determine if you must "reverse" [R] or if you will stress "unity" [U].)		(Express it in terms of a percentage.)
1. _____	fear	fear	R/U	1. ___%
	friendship	friendship	R/U	
	pride	pride	R/U	
	awkwardness	awkwardness	R/U	
	protectiveness	protectiveness	R/U	
	love	love	R/U	
2. _____	hate	hate	R/U	2. ___%
	harmony	harmony	R/U	
	pity	pity	R/U	
	defensiveness	defensiveness	R/U	
	embarrassment	embarrassment	R/U	
	rejection	rejection	R/U	
3. _____	inclusion	inclusion	R/U	3. ___%
	peacefulness	peacefulness	R/U	
	cooperation	cooperation	R/U	
	nervousness	nervousness	R/U	
	surprise	surprise	R/U	
	horror	horror	R/U	

4. _____	shock	shock	R/U	4. ___%
	serenity	serenity	R/U	
	receptivity	receptivity	R/U	
	vulnerability	vulnerability	R/U	
	anger	anger	R/U	
	tension	tension	R/U	
	happiness	happiness	R/U	
5. _____	anxiety	anxiety	R/U	5. ___%
	loyalty	loyalty	R/U	
	patriotism	patriotism	R/U	
	melancholy	melancholy	R/U	
	excitement	excitement	R/U	
	joy	joy	R/U	
	contentment	contentment	R/U	
6. _____	grief	grief	R/U	6. ___%
	resentment	resentment	R/U	
	irritation	irritation	R/U	
	confidence	confidence	R/U	
	isolation	isolation	R/U	
	other _____	other _____	R/U	
	other _____	other _____	R/U	
7. _____	other _____	other _____	R/U	7. ___%

The Harvard Yardstick

Harvard University research has found there are certain universal traits that all outstanding salespeople (in other words, outstanding persuaders) possess:

- **Perseverance.** Effective persuaders don't give up at the first raised eyebrow, the first voiced objection, or the first sign of rejection.

- **Willingness to accept consequences.** Successful persuaders don't blame others when things go wrong. They are secure enough to look inside, see what they did wrong, and resolve to do things better the next time.

- **Drive.** Those who are part of the persuasion brotherhood or sisterhood aren't apathetic. Instead, they possess an above-average motivation to convince others of the worth of a particular product or idea.

- **Ability to see another viewpoint.** High-performing salespeople can view a situation from a perspective other than their own.

- **Ability to set goals.** Every persuasive encounter should have a clearly determined goal. Overall, the determined persuader has a sense of what the individual goal will lead to in the long run.

- **Honesty.** Effective persuaders tell the truth—to themselves and to those they're trying to persuade. The effort required of the listener is carefully portrayed, as are the hoped-for results.

- **Willingness to approach strangers.** It's not always possible to know the people you wish to sell your concept to. Excellent salespeople aren't deterred by the prospect of working with strangers.

Read back through the list again, noting which attributes you possess. Were you able to relate four or more to your own persuasion process? If so, you're well on the way to becoming an effective and persuasive communicator.

Universal Questions

In any persuasive situation, the audience will have questions, which may or may not be articulated during the actual persuasion situation. The most successful persuaders are prepared to answer not only the questions that are voiced but also those that remain unexpressed. (You often will hear effective persuaders say, "Some of you may be thinking…")

Just as there are certain interview prompts that invariably are spoken ("Tell me about yourself"), there are certain questions that listeners invariably ask. If you prepare your responses ahead of time, you'll be ready to answer those questions.

Anticipating Questions Before They're Asked

A. Describe a situation in which you'd like to motivate someone to do something.

If a persuasion situation does not come readily to mind, try one of the following:

1. You would like to persuade a prospective client to use your product.

2. You would like your boss to hire temporary help for certain periods when the workload is excessive.

3. You would like to change your title.

4. You are eager to take on new responsibilities and would like to convince your boss that you can handle higher-level tasks.

I would like _____ to do the

following _____

_____

_____

under these conditions _____

_____

_____

_____

B. Now answer the following questions the audience might have regarding the situation you chose.

1. What is the cost? (Keep in mind that cost can refer to terms other than financial.) _____

_____

_____

2. How will the status quo be affected? _____

_____

_____

3. How much time will it take?_____

_____

_____

4. Why should I trust you? _____

_____

_____

_____

5. How do we know it will work? _____

_____

_____

_____

6. Who else is doing it? _____

_____

_____

7. How does it relate to what I need? _____

_____

_____

8. What's in it for me? _____

_____

_____

9. Why is this better than what we're already doing (or what we already have)? _____

_____

_____

_____

10. What are the long-term results? _____

_____

_____

_____

11. What could go wrong? _____

_____

_____

_____

12. How does the organization itself profit from this? _____

_____

_____

_____

P.E.R.S.U.A.D.E.

Universal Objections

If persuasion were an easy task, no books or seminars ever would have been developed around this topic. The fact is, persuasion skills take time to develop. You must constantly refine them. When you're successful, you actually convince others to do something they were initially reluctant to do. But getting them from reluctant to receptive is a question of overcoming objections.

Here are some universal objections you must be prepared to surmount:

1. I/we don't need this plan/product.

2. It's been tried before and it didn't work.

3. I don't think I could get the approval I'd need.

4. It's too risky.

5. It works fine the way it is.

6. Nobody would support it.

7. Let me think about it. I'll get back to you on it.

8. It will be more trouble than it's worth.

9. It's not feasible at this time.

10. We're not ready for it.

Overcoming Universal Objections

Using the same scenario you did in Exercise #18, tell how you would overcome each of the following objections:

1. I/we don't need this plan/product. _____

_____

_____

2. It's been tried before and it didn't work. _____

_____

_____

3. I don't think I could get the approval I'd need. _____

_____

_____

4. It's too risky. _____

_____

_____

5. It works fine the way it is. _____

_____

_____

6. Nobody would support it. _____

_____

_____

7. Let me think about it. I'll get back to you on it. _____

_____

_____

8. It will be more trouble than it's worth. _____

_____

_____

9. It's not feasible at this time. _____

_____

_____

10. We're not ready for it. _____

_____

_____

Universal Body Language

In addition to the questions that will be asked and the objections that will be raised, attune yourself to your audience's *nonverbal* messages. Here are but a few gestures and mannerisms for you to be aware of as you observe your audience. These actions can mean you're on the verge of losing your audience and therefore need to switch your approach. Keep adding to the list, if possible, so you can sharpen your sensitivity to what the silent messages might be telling you.

Area of Body	Negative Reaction
Face	• Eyes glazed over
	• Audience avoids eye contact
	• No acknowledgment (e.g., a head nod)
	• Audience looks around room, as if bored
	• Audience seems stone-faced to you yet smiles at others
	• You see or hear listeners yawn often
Hands	• Frequently looks at watch or the clock
	• Fingers tapping impatiently on table or desk
	• Playing with small objects
	• Hand-outs are accepted reluctantly and are glanced at quickly

Arms	• Crossed arms
	• Listener holds or reads newspaper as you are speaking
Legs	• Legs crossed
	• Impatient foot-tapping or shaking of legs
	• Listener frequently crosses and uncrosses legs
Whole body	• Listener isn't sitting on the edge of his or her seat
	• Listener's body is too relaxed, suggesting detachment, lack of interest

Taken alone, a given gesture may be misinterpreted. But if an audience member does it repeatedly, or if a *number* of audience members display it, or if it's being done in conjunction with other gestures that signal the same message, you'd do well to heed what you're being told. Your audience may be telling you that your persuasive attempt is failing.

Summary Exercise

Here are this chapter's key points about the universal aspects of persuasive messages. What do you remember (try not to look back) about each of the terms listed?

1. Describe the process involved in the Universal Reversal chart.

_____

_____

_____

_____

2. How many of the seven attributes that are universally shared by effective persuaders do you remember from the Harvard Yardstick?

_____

_____

_____

_____

_____

_____

_____

_____

_____

P.E.R.S.U.A.D.E.

3. How many of the twelve universal questions can you remember?

_____

_____

_____

_____

_____

_____

_____

_____

_____

_____

4. Which of the universal objections stand out in your mind?

_____

_____

_____

5. List some of the nonverbal ways listeners show they aren't being persuaded.

_____

_____

_____

Six

Anticipated

If you can anticipate your audience's reactions to your ideas, particularly those that may be negative, you can prepare a good defense.

The T-I-P Technique

"The unexamined life," the ancient Greeks pointed out, "is not worth living." Similarly, the unexamined persuasion is not worth delivering. The examination should include an anticipation of the reactions, objections, questions, and perhaps even the preconceptions your audience is likely to have.

One technique that forces consideration of these elements is the T-I-P technique. Outlining the answers to the questions prompted by each of these letters should help you prepare a solid argument.

T = Topic

Ask yourself: "What, exactly, is the topic here?"

"What is my main focus?"

"What is the essence of this persuasion effort?"

I = Information Needed

Ask yourself: "What information is needed by the other person?"

"What information may change perceptions and preconceptions?"

"What information will answer questions the audience may have?"

"What information will help the audience decide in my favor?"

"What information will overcome objections my audience might have?"

P = Point

Ask yourself: "What is the point?"

"How can I push, prod, or prompt the audience to accept that point?"

"What do I want my audience to do?"

"What final message do I want to leave with them?"

P.E.R.S.U.A.D.E.

Practice using the T-I-P technique with the following situation:

Assume you are preparing a memo for your boss. You are seeking approval for a guest speaker to address fellow engineers about "robust engineering." You've found there is considerable interest among your colleagues. Plus, a professor from a nearby university has agreed to deliver a lunchtime lecture at no charge.

Using the "T = Topic" prompt, you probably would note the following about the opportunity:

- Everyone is interested.

- It parallels corporate emphasis on continuous learning.

- The group needs to know more about this topic.

Considering the "Information Needed" prompt, you might jot down these thoughts:

- The boss always worries about cost—emphasize the fact that the professor will speak at no charge.

- The boss might say "no" because there's no room available, but the conference room is free for October 8, the day the speaker is tentatively scheduled.

- He's always worried about doing things "on company time"— remind him the speaker would be scheduled at lunchtime.

- Emphasize the high level of interest.

- Ask the boss to submit suggestions to upper management for an ongoing program.

Considering the "P = Point" prompt, your first-draft outline might include these comments:

- Once he gives approval, I will send out the memo—there'll be nothing for him to do.

- Maybe say, "Unless I hear from you to the contrary, I'll proceed with scheduling this first lecture on October 8."

- Invite him to attend.

Applying the T-I-P Technique

Using the notes from the sample outline about the T-I-P technique, write your memo in the space below.

_____

_____

_____

_____

_____

_____

_____

_____

_____

_____

_____

_____

_____

_____

_____

_____

_____

Anticipate Initial Curiosity

Whether your audience rejects, accepts, or remains neutral to the points you're trying to make, they will be curious—if only for the first few minutes—about what you have to say. Now is the time to engage them by aligning their interests (the old WIFM factor) with your intent. Here are ten ways to help your audience view you favorably— assuming they aren't carrying the old baggage of preconceived notions. (If they've made up their minds even before you begin, you'll have to work extra hard to win them over.)

1. **"Have you ever wondered why..."** If the question you ask next probes a mystery of corporate life or a common problem, you'll find your audience nodding in agreement with you. (The opening, naturally, must have direct relevance to the plan you're about to propose.) With this line, you'll be satisfying their curiosity about you and showing that you share mutual concerns.

2. **"In the words of our CEO..."** Quoting a well-loved or much-respected figure is one way to offset the initial reluctance some people will have. By stating immediately that you share in their admiration of this person, you can begin very early to build the bonds you'll need later to execute the plan. If you quote a person who's part of senior management, you're indirectly showing an alignment in thinking and are implying support for the proposal.

3. **"I have good news for you and bad news. Which do you want first?"** If you're making a speech, you could next ask for a show of hands. (An interactive request like this builds immediate rapport with an audience, giving them something to *do* other than passively listen to you.) If you're presenting the plan in writing, then your second sentence would not be a question but rather a declarative statement: "First, the bad news."

4. **"*Are you tired of...*"** Again, if you have chosen the "tired of" thing wisely, you will be able to move through several layers of skepticism, indifference, and tedium. If the topic is one that matters to your audience, they will listen closely to what you are offering as a solution to the problem.

5. **"*Did you know that...*"** These few words permit a segue into a startling statistic or fact of organizational life. Select a fact that will surprise your audience, guaranteeing extended interest and prompting them to ask the natural question, "So what are you going to do about it?" From the data-driven arousal of interest, you can proceed to explain your proposed solution, inviting the audience's participation along the way.

6. **"*I'd like to share with you something that happened to me...*"** Research has shown repeatedly that when speakers disclose a personal incident, they immediately establish a connection with their audience. This technique works better with spoken presentations, which allow more time and a more casual approach. However, if done well, the technique works with written presentations too.

   Divulging an actual life experience gives the audience an insight into the kind of person you are and into the forces that have shaped your life. In a sense, they feel privileged that you have chosen to share a private happening. As a rule, an audience feels a sense of reciprocity and will want to do something in return.

   You should ask several trusted friends or colleagues about the appropriateness of your selection prior to including it in your presentation.

7. **"*Reggie Jackson would give you the shirt off his back. Of course...*"** Humor often backfires because persuaders aren't usually as funny as they think they are. Unless you're a master joketeller, avoid attempts at being funny. Instead, tell a story that warms the heart, produces a wry or reminiscent smile, or serves as inspiration. It can be lighthearted—in fact, it might even stimulate guffaws—but it should be more anecdotal than the usual joke.

The Reggie Jackson line could work like this:

> *According to Catfish Hunter, "Reggie Jackson would give you the shirt off his back. Of course, he'd call a press conference to announce it!" Today, I'm not going to ask for the shirt off your back. I'm only asking for a few minutes of your time.*

8. **"*In the newspaper today, I saw...*"** Citing an account that appeals to common emotions brings a solid relevance, and immediacy to your message. You will be tapping into a much-discussed issue, one in which your audience might already have interest. This assumes you find an article relevant to your proposal.

An audience always has some degree of curiosity in a writer or speaker. Referring to a current event discloses that you, too, are troubled or pleased about what's happening in your community or nation or world.

9. **"*Those of us who...*"** These words grant you entry into the circle of those who support a certain stance or hold particular views. You can say directly to an audience that you in fact are "one of those who..."—just as they themselves are. Of course, it's possible that not everyone in your audience will share your philosophy, but you can choose a topic that is virtually all-inclusive. For instance: "Those of us who love this country..."

10. **"_____! For too long, we have allowed this belief to control our perceptions."** This opening is a bit of a shocker, but there are circumstances that call for shock (sometimes it's the only way to overcome complacency). When you shatter a myth, or challenge or shift paradigms, you're bound to arouse strong feelings in your audience—not necessarily feelings of agreement, but definite interest in what you have to say.

Using Your Opening to Address the Audience's Expectations

1. Whom will you need to influence in the near future?_____

   _____

2. On what issue? _____

   _____

   _____

   _____

   _____

   _____

3. Select one of the preceding openings and use it to satisfy the curiosity you expect to have from your audience. In addition to telling them a bit about you, use the opening to increase their receptivity to your message. _____

   _____

   _____

   _____

   _____

   _____

Moods in Question (Form)

Another area to anticipate before you begin any persuasive communication is the mood of your audience.

Typically, your audience's mood can be characterized in one of three ways:

- *Resistant* to your persuasive efforts, ready to challenge or to display apathy.

- *Neutral* in terms of caring one way or the other.

- *Accepting*, due to predisposition or the power of your persuasion.

Given these moods, you can logically anticipate typical questions your audience will have and then plan how best to answer the question—and perhaps even alter the mood.

Before your next persuasive effort, answer the questions in the chart on page 126. Doing so should boost your self-confidence and help you be better prepared to handle your audience.

The three moods do not change. No matter what your point is or who your audience is, you can anticipate one of these reactions. However, it's possible the questions will vary and thus your approach will as well.

Anticipating and Dealing With the Mood of Your Audience

Mood	Type of Question You Can Expect	Possible Approach to Use
Resistant	Why should we bother?	Logical presentation
	What good will this do?	Benefit-laden account
	What proof do you have it will work?	Data-driven evidence
Neutral	What are the pros and cons?	Detailed, visual depiction
	Will management approve it?	Endorsements from those above
	Do we have the resources available?	Financial feasibility
Accepting	What can we do to help?	Breakdown of who will do what
	Who else should we tell?	Implementation plan
	When do we start?	Projected time lines

P.E.R.S.U.A.D.E.

Anticipating Your Audience's Mood

Think of a situation from either your personal or your professional life that calls for you to be persuasive. Before preparing your statements, think of the moods that might prevail among audience members. Prepare questions of your own and note the approach that would be most convincing.

1. Explain the circumstances of the situation. _____

   _____

   _____

2. Determine the audience mood, questions you can expect, and possible approaches.

Mood	Type of question you can expect	Possible approach to use
Resistant	_____	_____
	_____	_____
	_____	_____
Neutral	_____	_____
	_____	_____
	_____	_____
Accepting	_____	_____
	_____	_____
	_____	_____

Summary Exercise

Here are the key points from this chapter about the need to anticipate what your audience may be thinking. What do you remember (try not to look back) about each of the terms listed?

1. Explain how to use the T-I-P technique. Specifically discuss each aspect of it.

"T"

_____

_____

_____

"I"

_____

_____

_____

"P"

_____

_____

_____

2. Anticipate initial curiosity. There are numerous openings that will pique audience interest. How many opening lines can you remember?

_____

_____

_____

_____

_____

_____

3. Moods in question. What do you recall about:

• Types of moods?

_____

_____

_____

• Examples of questions that reflect various moods?

_____

_____

_____

• Possible approaches to offset the questions above?

_____

_____

_____

Seven

Developed

No matter how convincing you think your argument is, it will lose its impact if you just toss your ideas out to the audience and hope they'll connect with something. In this chapter, you'll examine some effective methods for organizing your persuasive communications.

Subordination

The persuader with more "wins" than "losses" is the one who understands how a carefully developed argument can positively impact an audience. Two different persuaders—using exactly the same set of facts—can make two entirely different presentations. The more polished persuader will have subordinated the less important facts and will have prominently cited the more valuable. Putting your best verbal foot forward—a good definition for "subordination"—often allows you to get a foot in the door of resistance.

To see how subordination works, assume the following classified ad had been placed in the April 4 edition of the *Anytown Advocate*, your local newspaper:

Available: CORPORATE COMMUNICATIONS POSITION

We need an editor for our in-house publication; prefer an English major with three years of experience in this field and someone who has published articles or books. Write letter explaining why we should hire you.

Assume that both candidates applying for this position have the same background and experience:

- Both are English minors, not majors.

- Both have two years of experience.

- Both are writing a book, although neither has published.

Now, read the following letters and consider which candidate is more likely to be hired, based on the persuasive development of his or her letter. Note the strong and weak points of each argument.

Candidate "A"

I saw your ad for a corporate communications position as an editor for your company newspaper in the April 4 issue of the *Anytown Advocate*. My career goal is to become an editor of an in-house publication and so this job would be ideal for me.

I was not an English major but I was an English minor. I do not have three years experience—I have only two. I have not published anything but I am working on a book. I know I do not have an exact match for the qualifications you are seeking, but I come close. I would be happy to come in for an interview.

Candidate "B"

I believe my background and experience make me an ideal candidate for the corporate communications position advertised in the April 4 issue of the *Anytown Advocate*.

As an English minor, I took three journalism courses, which would serve me well in this position. For the past two years, I worked as a reporter for the *Pittsford Gazette*. Our editor, Jon Smith, will serve as a reference. Please call him at 555-2343 if you wish to know more about the quality of my work.

Currently, I am writing a nonfiction book about corporate communications. Although I do not yet have a publisher, I have had initial reviews that are quite positive. (A chapter is included for your review.)

Please call if you'd like to set up an interview (555-2644). I would be available any morning next week.

Candidate "A" probably feels she has a well-developed letter because it logically addresses each of the points solicited in the ad. It is well-developed in that sense, but it lacks the persuasive power shown in the response of Candidate "B." Notice that every sentence in the first letter begins with the word *I* or *My*. There is absolutely no sensitivity to or awareness of the other person (or company, in this case).

By beginning the letter by telling about the ad, "A" wastes the chance to start off with a strong lead. (The information should be included, but it should be subordinated, put into a less-important place.) "A" then goes on to discuss her personal goals rather than why she would be a good "fit" for the company that's placed the ad.

The next problem is that she directly admits she doesn't have the qualifications or experience the company seeks. Please understand: "subordination" does not mean lying. It *does* mean putting your better foot forward and not tripping yourself up.

Finally, Candidate "A" ends the letter by leaving the reader (and herself) hanging because there's no call to action. She doesn't say what she *wants* to happen next.

By comparison, Candidate "B" begins on solid, sure footing. He confidently states that he would be a good match for the person described in the ad. (Note the word *I* begins only one sentence.) The reference to the ad *is* mentioned but has been subordinated to follow the more important information about "my background and experience."

Subordination occurs again when the English minor aspect is acknowledged but not emphasized. What influences the reader is the fact that the candidate has taken journalism courses; details give further weight to the candidate's credentials. He mentions where he's currently working, gives a reference, and then explains the nature of his book.

The fact that he's not published "yet" (implying that he fully expects to be published one day) is subordinated in the "although" clause. This allows the reader to move rapidly to the more salient point: the reviews have been quite positive. If you believed your writing had merit, it would be a good idea to include it (in a situation such as this) for the potential employer to see.

P.E.R.S.U.A.D.E.

The "you" attitude is quite apparent here. The writer makes it convenient for the reader to call him and the reference. And the letter ends with a call to action: the writer tells the prospective employer to call and suggests that an interview should be the next step in this process.

You can see that "B" tells the same truths that "A" did. However, the facts presented by "B" are much more persuasive.

The 5-C Technique

As you well know by now, there are several effective approaches you can take to carefully develop your persuasive arguments. One of these approaches is the "5-C Technique." In addition to being easy to remember, the 5-C Technique lends cohesion to your points.

1st "C" = Compliment

The compliment can take the form of an expression of gratitude ("Thank you for taking the time from your busy schedules to attend this meeting") or a sincere tribute ("This team is known for asking tough questions and providing penetrating insights. That's what I'd like from you today—questions as tough as you can make them, insights as penetrating as they can be.")

The first "C," the "Compliment," works especially well in a spoken persuasion to warm the audience up.

2nd "C" = Contradict or Challenge

This step is intended to pique your audience's interest, to rock the boat of stereotypic thinking. You will not use the 5-C Technique for every persuasive situation, but you will use it when you want to introduce change or wake up complacent thinkers.

This second step asks you to contradict—prevalent thinking, existing mind-sets, or traditional practices. This approach is bold and forceful and works best when you're introducing a dramatic message. Here's the place to shatter a myth. You know, of course, that when you do, you'll gain greater visibility than you now enjoy. (Be prepared, though, for the disagreement that myth-shattering inevitably evokes.)

3rd "C" = Connect

In this middle stage, your job is to connect the new idea to old realities, to show how the seeming paradoxes aren't paradoxical at all (or, if they are, to show how your audience can live with them). By now, you will have stirred up your audience (and their minds) a bit. That's good. Ralph Waldo Emerson knew that when he advised: "A foolish consistency is the hobgoblin of little minds."

It's your job as a leader to occasionally disrupt thoughts. Remember, though, that you have an obligation to show how the new thinking actually fits into the existing structures of the organization.

4th "C" = Coordinate

Because traditional moorings of thought erode with the 5-C technique, you must put together a plan that offers security. If people are to follow your lead, they must know that the road is not impossibly long and the goal not impossibly difficult to achieve.

In this section of persuasive planning, you will note what efforts need to be coordinated and who will work with whom to do what by when. "What comes next?" is the question this step answers.

5th "C" = Culture-ize

Using the 5-C Technique, you can conclude your persuasive communication by showing how your proposal fits into the existing culture and improves upon it. This final step brings your proposal back to solid ground—the "bird's eye" perspective has changed from the big picture of possibility to a smaller picture that's "closer to home." This is the place to remind your audience that what you propose is not only doable, but also an extension of the organization's values, mission, or culture.

To see the 5-C approach in action, consider the following example. Assume you're a manager eager to encourage your supervisors to attend voluntary training programs. The resistance comes from a conviction that these supervisors (some of whom have been in supervisory roles for twenty years or more) already know their jobs well. You have allotted five minutes at the next staff meeting to make your pitch.

The 5-C Technique in Action

Compliment: The manager indirectly acknowledges the hard job employees have to do.

> *Before we tackle the tough issues that face us every week, I want to take a few minutes to tell you about an opportunity available to all of us.*

Contradict: The manager is sure to get their attention now.

> *I know you describe yourselves as "supervisors." But the truth is, you no longer supervise. The word literally means "looking over." And in the old days, supervisors did just that—they watched everything employees were doing. Today, however, things have changed. Ten percent of our workforce is telecommuting—we see them only once a week. And those who are still here are working in self-directed work teams.*

Connect: Constancy is stressed here, albeit a different kind.

The supervisor's role is still an important one, but it has changed. And we have to change to keep up with it. We must update our skills—all of us—to remain competitive. What we're already doing we're doing well and that won't change. What will change is the way we relate to the workforce, which is itself changing. We are becoming less "boss-like" and more "coach-like."

Coordinate: Provide the details and cite the benefits indirectly.

There is a new course available to us—at no charge. It will be held on four Friday mornings next month, on company time. The team and vendor meetings you usually have on Friday mornings will be eliminated those four days.

Culture-ize: The harsh realities of the company culture are noted, as is the reality that updated skills are valued in every culture.

None of us knows what the future has in store—the company is still downsizing. That's why I strongly encourage you to take advantage of this opportunity to sharpen your existing skills and pick up some new ones. Even if the worst does happen and you find yourself having to work at a different firm, the extra training will make you more valuable as a supervisor. No matter where you're working, these new skills will make your job easier.

P.E.R.S.U.A.D.E.

Putting the 5-C Approach to Work

A. Begin by thinking of a situation you think should change. The change may come as a surprise to your listeners, who may be quite satisfied with the status quo. Describe the change that should be effected: _____

_____

B. Now, using the five Cs, develop an argument to convince your audience to leave the old behind and embrace the new.

Compliment: _____

_____

_____

_____

_____

_____

Contradict or Challenge: _____

_____

_____

_____

_____

_____

_____

Connect: _____

_____

_____

_____

_____

_____

_____

Coordinate: _____

_____

_____

_____

_____

_____

_____

Culture-ize: _____

_____

_____

_____

_____

_____

_____

Parallelism

As you sharpen your persuasive edge, you make a greater impact. In the "D = Developed" part of P-E-R-S-U-A-D-E, you are consciously deciding—not so much *what* you will say but how you will say it. You may choose to develop within a given sentence by using subordination or within the entire message by using the 5-C Technique (or one of the others you have learned).

You can choose, too, to turn your developmental eye to the structure of a given paragraph. One technique that works well is called *parallelism*. It refers merely to the repetition of a particular word, phrase, or structure within a given passage. When Lincoln spoke of government, for instance, as being "of the people, by the people, and for the people," he employed parallelism. In this case, prepositions (*of, by, for*) introduced the three phrases, which all ended in *the people*.

Consistency is important in parallelism, as is audience awareness that the parallel structure is deliberate, not careless or inadvertent repetition. To illustrate, some would-be job applicants fill out application questions in the following manner (italics added for emphasis):

- *I have worked* as a secretary for ten years.
- *I have taken* numerous courses to upgrade my skills.
- *I have extensive* knowledge of computer systems.
- *I enjoy* interfacing with customers.

As you can see from the example, the responses are boring and repetitious. The applicant merely provides a listing of qualifications, with every sentence beginning with the word *I*. This is not parallelism; it is poor writing.

Because it packs a powerful stylistic punch, parallelism should be used judiciously. It would not be appropriate for a job application form, but it would be appropriate in situations calling for persuasion or inspiration.

Observe how President Ronald Reagan used it in his Inaugural Address of January 21, 1985 (italics added for emphasis).

We asked things of government that government was not equipped to give.

We yielded authority to the national government that properly belonged to the states or to local governments or to the people themselves.

We allowed taxes and inflation to rob us of our earnings and savings, and watched the great industrial machine that had made us the most productive people on Earth slow down and the number of unemployed increase.

We believed then and now: There are no limits to growth and human progress when men and women are free to follow their dreams.

In the earlier example involving the job applicant, the repetition of opening words was careless and inadvertent. Here, the parallelism is deliberate and developed. Can you see the difference?

Summary Exercise

Here are this chapter's key points about the development evident in persuasive messages. What do you remember (try not to look back) about each of the terms listed?

1. Describe how Candidate B effectively used subordination in his response to the classified ad.

   _____

   _____

   _____

   _____

2. How many of the Cs do you remember from the 5-C Technique?

   _____

   _____

   _____

   _____

   _____

   _____

   _____

   _____

   _____

   _____

3. Can you define the word *parallelism* and give an example of it?

_____

_____

_____

Eight

Energizing

Just as any persuasive communication should conclude with a call to action, so too does this book. This chapter provides several ways to energize your audience and inspire them to action.

Hard Words Versus Soft Words

It has been said that "only the persuaded can persuade." If your words, actions, gestures, and voice lack excitement, your audience can hardly become excited about your message. As you seek to involve, capture, and entice your readers or listeners, choose your words carefully. The final thrust of your persuasion is not the place for trite, timid, or tired words. Here you need words that make a declaration, words that shout and stomp and assert their own importance. You need "hard" words.

Look at the following two columns of words. Notice how the words in the first column tend to march proudly along, while those in the second column simply crawl.

outstanding	lovely
10 o'clock sharp	10-ish
want	interested in
has customer appeal	adorable
You misunderstood me.	Forgive me. I didn't mean to imply that.

"Hard" words are vital to persuasive communications because they involve your listeners and readers. Paul Verlaine advised writers to "take eloquence and wring its neck." There is a place for eloquence, but it's typically not in a persuasive argument that needs power to propel it straight to the audience's heart and mind. This is a job for hard words!

Exercise #24:

Hard Words Versus Soft Words

A. In the following selection, the soft words appear in boldface with a line beside them. In the blank spaces, write a hard word or phrase—one that has greater energy, one that will transmit that energy to your audience.

The Ishikawa or fishbone diagram is a **helpful** _____, easy-to-use analytical tool. It not only helps groups solve problems but also helps "create" problems. In other words, the process of **looking at** _____ causes and their effects **encourages** _____ us to consider something that "ain't broke" and **think of** _____ ways to prevent it from becoming broken. It also **allows** _____ us to have contingency plans ready for when the breakdown occurs. This tool **surely** _____ drives us to make the process **better** _____ than it currently is.

Answers

Instead of *helpful,* try *excellent* or *practical.*

Instead of *looking at,* try *examining* or *analyzing.*

Instead of *encourages,* try *forces.*

Instead of *think of,* try *consider* or *imagine.*

Instead of *allows,* try *impels* or *drives.*

Instead of *surely,* try *definitely.*

Instead of *better,* try *more efficient* or *more productive.*

B. Need a few more to practice on? Take a look at the following two openings and then the two closings.

The situation is this: a presentation was made to an audience, which included a prospective client. The client came up after the presentation, spoke a few words, and extended her business card.

The presenter wants to follow up by letter. Here are the opening and closing drafts.

Opening A   Dear Ms. Jones:

I'm glad you were in the audience today so we could speak—although briefly—about working together in the future.

Opening B   Dear Ms. Jones:

It was a pleasure to meet you today. I'm glad we could speak about the possibility of working together in the future.

Closing A   I have enclosed background material for your review. If you should have any questions, please do not hesitate to call me.

Closing B   The enclosed background materials will tell you more about the quality of my work. You will hear from me in the next several days—I'll call to see if we can arrange a lunch meeting to further discuss your training needs.

Which opening do you feel is fresher, more energetic, and more inviting? _____

Which closing provides a stronger call to action? _____

Answers

Opening A is the preferred opening.

- It uses a fresh phrase—"I'm glad you were in the audience" instead of the dull "It was a pleasure meeting you today."

- Opening A does not soften the possibility of future meetings by mentioning that it is only a possibility. Opening B weakens the reference to future work by qualifying it.

Closing B is preferable to Closing A.

- Closing A says "I have enclosed… " The sentence tells us little except that materials are enclosed, which the reader could see as soon as she opened the letter.

- Closing B makes the "enclosed materials" actually *do* something: they demonstrate the quality (important buzzword) of the work.

- Closing A leaves the reader hanging. There is nothing the reader is expected to do. There is no call to action.

- Closing B, by contrast, tells the reader what to expect. It also suggests that she look at her calendar for a possible lunch date.

Hard words shout; they don't whisper. They are bold and brazen. Above all else, they get noticed!

The A-B-Cs of Persuasion

A = Action

Action is the first ingredient in the A-B-C formula. Your words should demonstrate your willingness to take action (or give proof that you already have). Rhetoric alone will not suffice. Your words should also demand some action from your audience; they should energize, not weaken, others.

B = Believable

Listeners are more inclined to respond positively to your persuasive efforts when they believe you are telling the truth, sense they can trust you, and know that your intentions are honorable.

C = Catchy

One of the best devices you will ever find for making your words memorable is the *antimetabole*. As the prefix suggests, these are two forces working "against" each other, or going in opposite directions. (Aristotle wisely instructed: "We understand things when we view the opposite.") Meaning assumes a new (and sometimes original) clarity when it stands out in relief against an opposing concept. The antimetabole requires you to turn words around so each half of the turnaround creates an added dimension for both meanings.

Jesse Jackson, for example, once inspired an audience with these words, "I was born in the slums, but the slums were not born in me." And Ronald Reagan used an antimetabole in his Inaugural Address, titled "A Message of Hope": "That system has never failed us. But, for a time, we failed the system." Similarly, actress Jeanne Moreau created an unforgettable antimetabole: "Age doesn't protect you from love. But love, to some extent, protects you from age."

A-B-C Assessment

To obtain a quick sense of how well you apply the ABCs in your persuasive communications, answer the following questions with "True" or "False."

	True	False
1. I am described as "dynamic" from time to time.	___	___
2. This maxim could apply to me: "If you need something done, ask the busiest person you know."	___	___
3. I get bored quickly.	___	___
4. I am sensitive to the fact that others get bored quickly too.	___	___
5. This would never apply to me: "Ask her what time it is, and she'll show you how to make a watch."	___	___
6. I am known as a person of action.	___	___
7. People share secrets with me.	___	___
8. I believe I have high values and standards.	___	___
9. I have originated good puns on several occasions.	___	___
10. I enjoy learning about the English language.	___	___

Scoring: Clearly, the more "true" answers you had, the more energy your diction and delivery are likely to convey. A score of seven or more suggests you are a high-energy person, which is probably reflected by your speech.

To increase the energizing nature of your communications, consider the following;

1. Research has found that people who speak at a slightly faster rate are judged to be more believable than those who don't. Two hundred words per minute is an ideal rate—it keeps your audience rapt and virtually forbids them to daydream. To find what your normal rate is, count the words in a newspaper article, set a timer for two minutes, and then read the article aloud at your normal rate. When the timer goes off, mark your place and count the number of words.

   Another suggestion: ask a friend if you can tape record your next telephone conversation or casual meeting. (After a few moments, you will barely notice the recorder.) When the conversation has concluded, play the tape back and decide if your half of the discussion could be termed "lively," "funny," or even "interesting." Listen to the words you use, the details you include, and your intonation. If you score in the lower half of the "dynamic scale," seek advice from with those you respect or carefully observe people you would describe as dynamic.

2. At the end of your work days, how satisfied do you feel about what you've accomplished? If you can congratulate yourself, if you frequently receive praise from others, you probably are one of those "busy persons." If you get things done, your communications are probably direct, pointed, and deliberate. They probably state with great clarity what action is required of the audience.

P.E.R.S.U.A.D.E.

If not, you may need to attend time-management classes (or, at the very least, read some books on the topic). Organize your files and learn to prioritize.

3. If you do get bored quickly, it may be a good sign—a sign that you don't like to waste time, but instead like to spend it well. Your articulation probably reflects your need to be interested and interesting at the same time. These two needs constitute the basic thread of persuasion—you have a sincere interest in the problems and needs of others (the basic "you" attitude) *and* you meld their concern with your own to effect positive change.

4. Realizing that an audience can become quickly bored (there are those who believe you have only thirty seconds in which to sell yourself and your idea) forces you to get to the point and to make it pointed. Unlike those who are enthralled with the sound of their own voices, good presenters understand the urgency of delivering a crisp, clear, and convincing message. If you are energized, eager to get moving, and excited about prospects, these feelings are bound to spill over onto your audience.

5. Make an audiotape of yourself trying to persuade someone to do something. Also make several copies of communications you have sent to others you wished to influence. As you listen and read, note the excessive verbiage you use. (Don't confuse it with repetition, which can be a potent persuasive tool.) Some examples of excessive verbiage would be:

> *Vendor X is engaged in providing a range of office products.*

> Better: Vendor X provides office products.

> *A vote on the proposal was taken by the benchmarking team, and an affirmative outcome was the result.*

> Better: The benchmarking team voted to accept the proposal.

Another example is the person who creates tedium with tiresome details. Do you know people who sound like this? (Ideally, you're not such a person!)

Last Tuesday, I went to a meeting…wait a minute, it couldn't have been Tuesday because my boss was out of town on Tuesday and I never leave the office unattended when she's not there. So it must have been Monday, but come to think of it—we never have meetings on Monday, unless it's an emergency and we haven't had an emergency meeting since 1988 when the power outage occurred. Or was it 1989? No, it couldn't have been 1989 because that was the year I got my promotion and I remember once saying that when you're newly promoted, every day is a crisis but in truth, there were no major crises that year, so it must have been 1989 after all.

6. "Actions," we are told, "speak louder than words." If you can use words, you will have the stuff of which impressive persuasions are made. What proof can you offer of your commitment to a change you are proposing? What have you actually done (or are planning to do) to manifest your commitment to this project, plan, or proposal?

_____

_____

_____

_____

_____

_____

7. Your good name, some believe, is worth more than any asset. In all you do (at least in the business world), your reputation precedes you. Even in a job interview, when you're trying to persuade someone to hire you, you will usually be asked to supply references. If those references speak well of you and validate the claims you make about your own willingness to work hard, then your chances of obtaining the position are magnified.

   Past performance is a good predictor of future success. If others have found you believable in the past, they are more likely to trust you in the present, as you work to persuade them to "do it your way."

   Can you keep confidences? Do you engage in gossip? Are you a person of your word? The trust factor is critical for people attempting to persuade.

8. Life has us "on the go" virtually every moment of every day. As a result, it's difficult to find time for reflection. Often, the only time many people have available for introspection is during the process of learning—either in a class or with a book like this. Reflect now on the values you were raised with, the standards you have developed, and the beliefs you hold dear.

   Periodically ask yourself (and others) questions such as the ones in Exercise #25. They provide a moral anchor, enabling you to speak from the heart. Your audience will listen when you do.

9. Laughter is a great energizer. Even if you're not a naturally funny person, you do have a memory. Use it to record funny lines, anecdotes, and witticisms uttered by others (to whom, of course, you will always give credit). Quoting a deliciously funny or apropos remark creates almost the same impact as uttering your own.

10. Even if you aren't enamored of the words of your language, you can begin a love affair right now—assuming, of course, that you truly intend to become more persuasive than you already are. Experiment with words, play with them, put them in and take them out until you find the right ones that convey the energy, conviction, or inspiration that you need. Effective persuasion begins with trial and error, as shown in the words of author Vladimir Nabokov: "My pencils outlast their erasers."

Kinesthesia

On occasion, you will find that using the verbal technique of "kinesthesia" lends an intriguing twist to your persuasive message. Use it sparingly, but know that when it works, it really works. "Kinesthesia" refers to deliberately mixing the senses. The following question employs kinesthesia:

If you could taste anger, would it taste like sherbet or sandpaper?

In an oral persuasive presentation, kinesthesia can help you appeal not only to your audience's emotions but also to their senses. And the more appeals you make, the greater engagement you are likely to have.

Look at this example before attempting one of your own:

Our latest directive—if you could feel it, would it be more like something stuck in your craw, like a burr under your metaphoric saddle, or like a security blanket that protects? The policy was designed to provide security and yet we are hearing that some employees are troubled by it. I've called you together today so we can discuss our concerns.

Practicing Kinesthesia

Try your own now. Imagine some issue you would like to bring up with colleagues or family members or a friend: _____

_____

_____

Now involve their senses as you express the issue with a kinesthetic hypothesis ("If you could see…" or "If you could hear…" or "If you could smell…" or "If you could touch…" or "If you could taste…"): _____

_____

_____

_____

_____

_____

_____

Summary Exercise

Here are the key points from this chapter about energy in persuasive messages. What do you remember (try not to look back) about each of the items listed?

1. Hard words versus soft words

   _____

   _____

   _____

   _____

   _____

2. Ways to make your communications more lively, especially the openings and closings

   _____

   _____

   _____

   _____

   _____

   _____

   _____

3. What do the letters A, B, C stand for and what do they call for in your persuasive communications?

"A" _____

_____

_____

"B" _____

_____

_____

"C" _____

_____

_____

4. How many of the tips from the A-B-C Assessment can you recall?

_____

_____

_____

_____

_____

_____

_____

_____

5. How would you define *kinesthesia?* Can you give an example?

_____

_____

_____

_____

Conclusion

The letters in the word "P-E-R-S-U-A-D-E" will guide you as you prepare persuasive communications for personal and professional situations, formal and informal circumstances—messages designed to motivate others to answer a call to action. While there are many smaller strategies contained within each of the letters, the overall strategy is an umbrella that will protect you from forces seeking to drown your enthusiasm for the job to be done.

Exercise #27:

In conclusion, here are two persuasive messages, A and B. The situation is this: Senior management has asked for employee suggestions for speakers to "kick off" a new corporate program. Suggestions must be in writing and no longer than one page in length.

Message B reflects the eight aspects of the metastrategy you have learned:

      P = Positioned

      E = Engaging

      R = Realistic

      S = Simplified

      U = Universal

      A = Anticipated

      D = Developed

      E = Energizing.

Message A does not.

As you read Message A, use a "P" to indicate where positioning is needed, and "R" to show where the writing fails to be realistic, and so on. Then using your notes, write a paragraph critiquing the message and explaining why it failed.

As you read Message "B," do the same thing. Write appropriate letters (**P** for Positioned, **E** for Engaging, **R** for Realistic, **S** for Simplified, **U** for Universal, **A** for Anticipated, **D** for Developed, and **E** for Energizing) above the words or phrases that reflect the particular elements. Once you've outlined your thoughts using this method, write a complete analysis.

Message A

I want to propose an unusual speaker for our annual corporate kick-off event. I've made several other proposals, but naturally, no one has ever paid any attention to them. The choices made on Mahogany Row in the past haven't exactly been spectacular so maybe now it's time for an idea from the trenches. Whenever there is a kick-off, we have to listen to some high-ranking honcho drone on and on about productivity or quality or mission. I think we need a change. Let's go with a big-name athlete. Everyone likes sports and we can get some motivation, which we all need. So, I'd like to make a pitch for John Madden to speak to us. Whether or not you're a receiver, you have to agree we can all use a Hail Mary pass.

Your analysis (using the letters you noted in the text above)

_____

_____

_____

_____

_____

_____

_____

_____

_____

_____

_____

_____

_____

_____

_____

_____

_____

_____

_____

Message "B"

When asked how to stay in shape for the television football season, John Madden gave this advice: "Lie around a lot. A mistake some people make in the summer is to move around too much. Just practice sitting for six, seven, hey—ten or twelve hours. Do nothing. Then when you've got the sitting part down, it's easy to put the game there in front of you."

Not everyone likes football, but everyone likes to laugh. Local sportscaster Mad "N" Jonn has the same sense of humor as his namesake, and his fee is only $100.

Wry humor plus motivation for us to play "the great game of business"—what better way for us to kick off the project and move toward our goal line? I propose Mad "N" Jonn for these reasons:

He's available.

He's inexpensive.

He's funny and inspiring.

He's received rave reviews for other kick-offs.

Your analysis (using your letters and notes from the text):

Answers

Message A contains none of the elements of effective persuasion.

- *Positioned*   There is no evidence of carefully thought out or strategically placed points. Instead, the style seems to be "stream-of-consciousness"—the writer is saying whatever comes to mind. Putting a complaint and/or making a charge against the reader in the very first sentence of a persuasive message shows the writer has no understanding of the meaning of the word "positioning." And, it's not until the end of the message that the reader gets even a clue about the type of speaker the writer is proposing.

- *Engaging*   The language, with its direct insults and indirect insinuations, does not engage the reader. In fact, it disengages. There's no appeal to the reader's mind, emotions, or funny bones.

- *Realistic*   The memo overlooks reality in two ways. First, it's not likely the organization could afford to hire a big-name motivational speaker such as John Madden. Second, the writer isn't realistic when he asserts that "everyone likes football." Third, his assertion that they all need motivation is not only untrue, it's probably offensive to the many employees who are already motivated.

- *Simplified*   The basic thrust of the message is clouded by competing agendas here. Rather than a simple, straightforward suggestion—once or twice repeated—the writer goes off on several tangents. The clarity of the message is further obscured by the arcane references to football, which would be confusing to the non-football fan.

- *Universal*   On every count, the writer fails to entice the audience with allusions to commonly held views or emotions. He spends about half the reader's time spouting a litany of personal complaints—never very interesting and completely inappropriate in a persuasive effort.

- *Anticipated*   There's no indication whatsoever that the writer has thought ahead to likely questions or objections. And so there's no effort made to answer or overcome the issues that should have been anticipated.

- *Developed*   The writer makes only a random effort at development. He begins with a veiled proposal and then concentrates on himself for a while before jumping to past events and finally returning to the proposal. In the space of one paragraph, he addresses a number of issues—and the majority of them don't belong in the memo at all.

- *Energizing*   The reader feels dragged down by this memo rather than inspired, uplifted, or persuaded. The negativity virtually bounces off the page.

Other cardinal sins have been committed as well. The tone is whiny. The writer focuses on an agenda of complaint that has nothing to do with the proposal being sought. The tone is also accusatory and somewhat insulting. While the reader may have some tolerance for the "poor-me" attitude in the second sentence, even that tolerance disappears when the writer points to poor choices made "on Mahogany Row" (a phrase some would consider pejorative).

The mention of the word "trenches" creates a divide in sharp contrast to the whole purpose of the kick-off event (and the selection of a speaker for it)—harmony. Any chance at a positive reception for his message wanes when the writer makes negative comments about being bored by "high-ranking honchos" (some of whom may be reading the proposal). The tone continues to grate on the reader as it alludes to important themes like "quality" as being unimportant.

Conversely, Message "B" contains each of the factors considered integral to effective persuasions.

- *Positioned*

  From the onset, the writer demonstrates appreciation of the reader's interests. While not everyone is potato-couched during football season, everyone either lives with someone or knows someone who is. And so, the understated humor of the Madden quote penetrates the reader's consciousness and maintains a strong position.

  The very look of the memo is so much more inviting than the previous one. The paragraphs are short, and the listing of the benefits at the end positions the selling points quite clearly.

P.E.R.S.U.A.D.E.

Further, the phrase "his fee is only $100" is placed right after the opening quote, so the reader can continue with the memo without wondering whether price will be prohibitive.

- *Engaging* Quotations usually make a reader sit up and take notice, as this one does. Further allure can be found in the short sentences and the variety of sentence length. The paragraph after the quote contains the "meat" of the proposal, and it is clearly served to the reader.

- *Realistic* The writer acknowledges that not everyone likes football, and then obtains our concurrence by noting everyone does like to laugh. Further evidence of the realistic approach to the situation can be found in the author's getting the question of cost out of the way quickly.

- *Simplified* The language is simple—there's no arcane athletic jargon to confound the reader. The simple parallelism in the last four sentences ("He's available. He's inexpensive.") drives home the point. The reader is left feeling the proposed speaker is the ideal speaker.

- *Universal* The writer is aware of the universal appeal of laughter as well as the universal corporate concern about controlling costs. Both points are addressed expediently and in appropriate places.

- *Anticipated*

    The writer knows expense can prevent a good idea from being launched and dispels potential fear by mentioning the cost early in the memo. At the end, the writer addresses other potential objections, like availability and quality. The final selling point is the implicit guarantee that the organization will be pleased with this speaker, as others have used him and rave about his presentation.

- *Developed*

    Throughout this memo, there is proof that the writer used the most effective structure, proceeding from the "hook" into football and laughter. An effective transition is then made to the proposal of Jonn as the speaker.

    Citing the speaker's talents, the writer leads us to a mention of "the great game of business" (the title of a very popular business book by Jack Stack), which may be important to the managers reading the memo.

    The writer concludes the memo by restating the recommendation and by making four final persuasive points.

- *Energizing*   While football language is used in this memo, it is language the average reader probably is familiar with. The brevity of the final four lines propels the reader forward, building momentum of the syntax. The rhetorical question ("What better way...") elicits agreement that there's no better way to kick off the event than with Mad "N" Jonn.

Memo "B" is longer than "A," but it moves faster. The language generates a sense of energy.

Bibliography and Suggested Reading

Byrd, Richard. *Say the Magic Words*. New York: Berkley Publishing, 1993.

Caroselli, Marlene. *The Language of Leadership*. Amherst, MA: Human Resource Development Press, 1990.

Elgin, Suzette Haden. *BusinessSpeak: Using the Gentle Art of Verbal Persuasion to Get What You Want at Work*. New York: McGraw-Hill, 1995.

Elsea, Janet G. *The Four-Minute Sell*. New York: Simon and Schuster, 1984.

Henggeler, Paul. *Kennedy Persuasion: The Politics of Style Since JFK*. Chicago: I.R. Dee, 1995.

Hopkins, Tom. *How to Master the Art of Selling*. New York: Warner Books, 1982.

Karrass, Chester L. *The Negotiating Game*. New York: HarperCollins, 1992.

Martel, Myles. *The Persuasive Edge*. New York: Random House, 1989.

Peppers, Don. *Life's a Pitch: Then You Buy*. New York: Currency/ Doubleday, 1995.

Quick, Thomas L. *The Persuasive Manager*. Radnor, PA: Chilton Book Company, 1982.

Rusk, Tom. *The Power of Ethical Persuasion: From Conflict to Partnership at Work and in Private Life*. New York: Viking, 1993.

Spence, Gerry. *How to Argue and Win Every Time: At Home, at Work, in Court, Everywhere, Every Day*. New York: St. Martin's Press, 1995.

Tammemagi, Hans. *Winning Proposals: How to Write Them and Get Results*. North Vancouver: Self-Counsel Press, 1995.

Available From SkillPath Publications

Self-Study Sourcebooks

AIM First! Get Focused and Fired Up to Follow Through on Your Goals *by Lee T. Silber*

The Business and Technical Writer's Guide *by Robert McGraw*

Climbing the Corporate Ladder: What You Need to Know and Do to Be a Promotable Person
by Barbara Pachter and Marjorie Brody

Discovering Your Purpose *by Ivy Haley*

Going for the Gold: Winning the Gold Medal for Financial Independence *by Lesley D. Bissett, CFP*

Having Something to Say When You Have to Say Something *by Randy Horn*

The Innovative Secretary *by Marlene Caroselli, Ed.D.*

Mastering the Art of Communication: Your Keys to Developing a More Effective Personal Style
by Michelle Fairfield Poley

Organized for Success! 95 Tips for Taking Control of Your Time, Your Space, and Your Life
by Nanci McGraw

P.E.R.S.U.A.D.E.: Communication Strategies That Move People to Action *by Marlene Caroselli, Ed.D.*

Productivity Power: 250 Great Ideas for Being More Productive *by Jim Temme*

Promoting Yourself: 50 Ways to Increase Your Prestige, Power, and Paycheck
by Marlene Caroselli, Ed.D.

Risk-Taking: 50 Ways to Turn Risks Into Rewards *by Marlene Caroselli, Ed.D. and David Harris*

Speak Up and Stand Out: How to Make Effective Presentations *by Nanci McGraw*

Stress Control *by Steve Bell*

Total Quality Customer Service: How to Make It Your Way of Life *by Jim Temme*

Write It Right! A Guide for Clear and Correct Writing *by Richard Andersen and Helene Hinis*

Your Total Communications Image *by Janet Singe Olson, Ph.D.*

Spiral Handbooks

The ABC's of Empowered Teams: Building Blocks for Success *by Mark Towers*

Assert Yourself! Developing Power-Packed Communication Skills to Make Your Points Clearly,
Confidently, and Persuasively *by Lisa Contini*

Breaking the Ice: How to Improve Your On-the-Spot Communication Skills *by Deborah Shouse*

The Care and Keeping of Customers: A Treasury of Facts, Tips, and Proven Techniques for
Keeping Your Customers Coming BACK! *by Roy Lantz*

For more information, call 1-800-873-7545.

Notes

Notes